BRITISH TRAINING FOR AMERICAN RETRIEVERS

BRITISH TRAINING FOR AMERICAN RETRIEVERS

UNLEASH YOUR DOG'S NATURAL TALENT

VIC BARLOW

© 2003 Vic Barlow

Photo credits: **Gaynor Bailey** © 22, 135, 140, 155, 164, 176; **Norvia Behling** © 227; **Denver Bryan / denverbryan.com** © 25 (Labrador retrievers), 32, 34, 44, 58, 74, 120, 128, 133, 187, 192, 204, 205, 213, 223, 235; **Close Encounters of the Furry Kind** © 25 (golden retriever), 43, 67, 129, 211; **Kent & Donna Dannen** © 25 (flat-coated retriever), 241; **Tara Darling** © 122; **Cheryl Ertelt** © 30, 31, 181, 189; Jean Fogle © 40, 182, 246; **Ron Kimball Photography / ronkimballphoto.com** © 231; **Gary Kramer / garykramer.net** © 41, 108, 237; **Tim Robinson** © 15, 63, 64, 77, 79, 84, 86, 88, 94, 102, 105, 112, 124, 131, 139, 143, 146, 147, 150, 159, 161, 165, 169, 175, 178, 191, 200, 202, 207, 208, 220, 234; **Dusan Smetana** © 48, 54, 180, 224, 240, 247; **Dale C. Spartas / www.spartasphoto.com** © 13, 19, 25 (Chesapeake Bay), 45, 47, 51, 61, 75, 91, 98, 110, 116, 125, 184, 194, 195, 215, 243, 244; **Ben O. Williams** © 111, 198

All rights reserved. No part of this book may be reproduced or transmitted in any form by any means, electronic or mechanical, including photocopying, recording, or by any information storage and retrieval system, without written permission from the Publisher.

Published by Willow Creek Press
P.O. Box 147, Minocqua, Wisconsin 54548

Design and edit by Andrea Donner

Library of Congress Cataloging-in-Publication Data:
Barlow, Vic, 1955-
    The British training method for American retrievers / Vic Barlow.
       p. cm.
       ISBN 1-57223-597-7 (pbk.)
   1. Retrievers--Training--Great Britain. 2. Retrievers--Training--United States. I. Title.
    SF429.R4B37 2003
 636.752'735--dc21
                                                                  2003008861

Printed in the United States

Table of Contents

Foreword 7

Introduction 9

Chapter One: Setting Your Objectives 13

Chapter Two: The Pack Mentality 31

Chapter Three: Early Days 41

Chapter Four: Learning the Fundamentals 75

Chapter Five: Formal Retrieving 111

Chapter Six: Advanced Training 129

Chapter Seven: Dealing with Obstacles 165

Chapter Eight: Water Work 181

Chapter Nine: Quartering & Flushing 195

Chapter Ten: Your First Season 205

Chapter Eleven: General Health 227

Chapter Twelve: Problem Solving 241

Index 253

Acknowledgements

Indulge me if you will in this brief opportunity I have to thank Mike and Cathy Stewart of Wildrose Kennels in Oxford, Mississippi, for their friendship, kindness and wonderful Southern hospitality.

Neither must I forget Tupelo Deputy Police Chief Bill Gibson for leading me into all kinds of misadventures, or Steve Smith and Jake at The Retriever Journal for their unstinting encouragement and support.

Back home in England, I offer my sincere thanks to Ian and Wendy Openshaw, Bert Taylor, John Halstead, Chris Woods, Eileen Dudley, and Eileen Haworth who have given me the benefit of their vast canine experience without which none of this would have been possible.

Credit is due to the entire Bibby family who looked after my kennels whenever Uncle Sam called.

My wife Delma continued to be my wisest advisor and closest friend throughout the entire project and nothing I say will ever be enough to thank her.

Finally, I'd like to express my gratitude to Blue, Jess, Stan, Daz, Connie, Zulu, Charlie, Gabby, and all those other wonderful retrievers that did more for me than I had any right to expect.

Vic Barlow
Cheshire
England

FOREWORD

I don't know of anyone better equipped to discuss the British retriever with a bunch of Yanks than Vic Barlow. Or anyone with a more profound understanding of what it is that a retriever should do in the field without all the bells and definitely all the whistles.

There has long been a disconnect between the retriever training methods in the U.K. and in North America. The British manner, for many Americans and Canadians, makes more sense to them on a day-to-day basis because its aim is to produce a finished gun dog.

Vic is the U.K. Correspondent for *The Retriever Journal*, but I think he's in the States more than he is at home. And there's a good reason for it: He keeps getting called back by people who appreciate the way he trains trainers to turn dogs into steady, reliable, and companionable field performers. And Vic does it in a novel way – to the degree possible, he lets the dog be a dog instead of an extension of the handler's will and psyche, and he teaches it in the gentle, jolly, upbeat fashion of an accomplished storyteller.

One thing you will notice in this book is how the level of expectations in the British method differ from those in the States – does your dog whine and carry on in the blind and you chuckle at his intensity? In a U.K.-trained dog, that's unacceptable. But can your American dog do his work in the field with six or eight other dogs all going hither and yon at the same time, picking up bird after bird and not get confused or competitive? The British dogs do it daily. (Mine can't, by the way.)

Vic's methods are simplicity themselves because they are built on one very important precept: What does the dog really need to know to be a good performer for the gun? Everything else, as they say, is elaboration. His methods are built on common sense because they train for the situations your dog will see in the field or marsh, not for a once-in-a-lifetime blind quad on 300-yard ducks.

I think the thing you'll appreciate most about this book is the way Vic Barlow thinks like a retriever, anticipates what a dog will do in any situation, and uses skill and cunning to stay three steps ahead of the dog. I wouldn't be surprised if he shakes when he gets out of the shower.

Steve Smith
Editor, *The Retriever Journal*
Traverse City, Michigan

INTRODUCTION

I probably hold the British record for crossing the Atlantic. Last time I checked I had 81 U.S. immigration stamps plastered across my current passport. Most Brits want to visit Florida or shop the Big Apple, but not me. No, sir, I have other more important matters in hand. I have dogs to work, and not any old dogs you understand, but retrievers. Of course, I can appreciate the thrill of meeting Mickey and Minnie or the excitement of a Universal Studios Tour. I can almost comprehend the buzz some folks get from a charge card busting trip to Neiman Marcus, but for me, The Magic Kingdom is wherever those dogs are working.

Leaving England is always a wrench, due in no small part to the row of accusing eyes peering at me from inside the kennel block, but any guilt on my part is quickly assuaged by the wonderful welcome I always receive from American owners.

Initially, the depth of interest in British Retriever Training techniques surprised me; I had no idea they were any different than those employed in the U.S. It wasn't until I had attended my first American field Trial and Hunt Test that I began to appreciate the disparity. Some of the dogs I saw performing were truly sensational; an American field Trial is a thrilling event. Nowhere in England would I ever see a four-hundred-yard retrieve of any kind, or watch a dog complete a difficult swim down a narrow channel of water it could so easily avoid. What I witnessed was an incredible test of American handling techniques, but it told me very little about the natural ability of the dogs.

British Retriever Trials are primarily a test of the dog's skill as a game finder. Their training is simply a means of honing and developing that talent to its full extent. The British dog must retrieve game shot whenever and wherever it appears, delivering it softly to hand as quickly and quietly as possible. No two birds are ever shot in the same location. Just as in a hunt, every retrieve is a unique adventure.

It became obvious to me that while both British and American handlers were working the same types of dogs, the events for which they were being prepared could not be more different. Little wonder then that their respective training techniques vary so fundamentally.

The Brits are teaching their dogs to find *every* bird, while American handlers are training for an event in which tracking cripples plays no part. As all hunters know, birds do not always conveniently fall into the open. Many plunge into dense woodland or drift into reeds where the dog has no sight of his handler and must work entirely on his own initiative. British trial dogs are schooled for exactly this type of situation, but you will rarely see such a retrieve in an AKC Field Trial or Hunt Test.

That's why their respective training regimes are so fundamentally different and why Brit Dog is out in the field learning to use his nose on live game while his American cousin is "lining to a pile" or perfecting a "swim by."

At my regular U.S. workshops I see many wonderful retrievers which, given the correct training, could be exceptional hunting companions. But instead of feeling pride,

INTRODUCTION

their owners are awash with guilt at their dog's inability or unwillingness to behave like a television Trial dog.

It's my aim in this book to straighten things out. So if having a steady, quiet, reliable retriever is more relevant to you than winning the National, read on. If finding that difficult cripple is more important than owning the latest e-collar, this book is definitely for you.

Above all, working with your dog should be fun, so along the way I have retold a few true stories that'll make you smile.

In the following chapters you will find no drills involving e-collars, force fetch, force to a pile, or, come to think of it, "force" anything. All are unheard of in British Retriever Training.

For those of you brave enough to take "the path less traveled," the rewards for both owner and dog will be a revelation. Enjoy.

Chapter One
SETTING YOUR OBJECTIVES

My wife owns a large, male golden retriever. Max is a great, handsome brute bred from show stock and greatly admired by all the local ladies. In the daytime, he lays on the landing where he can observe his legion of female fans walking past the house. Astonishingly, some of them actually wave and he nods back in acknowledgement. If it's a girl he really likes, he will put his front paws on the windowsill and give her the full, fanned-tail treatment. Max knows how to turn it on. Mrs. B adores him and allows him all kinds of privileges forbidden to my working dogs.

One day last season a local hunting enthusiast desperate for canine company after losing his beloved Lab to a heart condition asked if he could borrow Max. Allowing her kind-hearted nature to overrule logic, Mrs. B agreed and packed Max off on his first hunting trip like a nervous mother sending her small child to summer camp.

She was told to expect him back by late afternoon, but he failed to return. By nightfall she was beginning to wonder if there had been some kind of traffic accident and nervously tuned in to the local television and radio stations for news.

Just as she was about to panic, a bedraggled figure crawled up the driveway oozing mud, accompanied by Max wagging his tail triumphantly.

"He ran off with the bag of birds," gasped our hunting enthusiast pointing at Max.

"The ones that he retrieved for you?" Enquired Mrs. B.

"Retrieved... Retrieved!" he exploded. "This dog couldn't retrieve his own tail."

"But he's a wonderful dog," Mrs. B protested.

"Wonderful, are you kidding? That dog's a free loader." The guy was starting to scream. "He's done nothing but eat, sleep, and pee all day," he yelled, now clearly out of control. "He even scared the ducks away with his snoring."

Max looked on proudly.

"Well, at least you got your birds back," said Mrs. B soothingly, but he continued to wail.

"I'll show you what I got back," and he produced what I can only describe as a sack of bloody feathers. "And I had to chase him all the way across the marsh to get these. I'm completely exhausted."

"Oh you poor man," said Mrs. B winking surreptitiously at Max. "I'll make you a nice pot of tea." (The standard British answer to all emergencies.)

When he had been fortified with hot tea, Scotch whiskey, and a generous slice of Mrs. B's fruitcake, he left for home still mumbling incoherently. He was obviously a soul in torment.

Max meanwhile chomped on his dinner contentedly and watched *Sex in the City* before falling into an untroubled sleep.

Chapter One: Setting Your Objectives

"That dog is a real embarrassment," I rapped. "All he ever does is follow you around the garden, flirt with your girlfriends, and sleep."

"And that's exactly what I want him to do," she replied. "Pity husbands don't always turn out as planned."

At six years of age, Max is exactly the kind of dog Mrs. B dreamed he would be when she bought him as a pup. It isn't an accident that he walks nicely to heel, is very gentle around children, never barks, shows not the slightest aggression, and treats the furniture with the utmost respect. Mrs. B has spent hours educating him to do just that. Max has fulfilled all the ideals she set for him.

So many owners start a training program without any clear objective. Had she wanted Max to be a working dog, her plans would have been doomed from the start. He was the wrong dog with the wrong genes, but fortunately that was not her plan. She groomed him from birth to be her "Pet Dog." The fact that Max has the retrieving instinct of a creosote post is irrelevant.

Mrs. B and Max, her "perfect" dog.

Is color or looks more important to you than temperament? Will you settle for an under-achiever if he looks good?

No one would buy a car without considering all their requirements and yet so many owners buy a pup without thinking carefully about its ultimate role. It isn't impossible to train any dog to retrieve, but it's a damn sight easier when you have a pup with the right pedigree.

Think very carefully about what you want from your dog when he's fully grown. Is color more important to you than temperament? Will you settle for an under-achiever if he looks good?

Year after year the line up for the British Retriever Championship is approximately forty-five black Labs, four yellow Labs, and a golden retriever. No chocolate Lab has ever made it to the final. Those statistics have to tell you something, but if performance is not your most important criteria, then it need not concern you.

Do you want a duck dog, an upland hunter, or both? Is he going to be a family pet or a totally dedicated working retriever? Make a determined effort to write down your

CHAPTER ONE: SETTING YOUR OBJECTIVES

objectives *before* you buy your pup. It can save you an awful lot of frustration.

Once you have your pup, you must work backwards from your objectives and ensure that what you do with him today doesn't undermine your ultimate goal. Unlike a computer, a pup has no delete button. You can't ask him to forget what he's been allowed to learn later when you don't like the results.

All my dogs are invited into the kitchen at some time, but no further. (Except for Max and Blue.) They know the house rules. It's no use expecting your dog to understand that he can wander around the house when he's clean and dry but not when he's wet and muddy; he won't comprehend. That kind of regime might work on husbands, but not on dogs (or kids).

Be sensible in what you expect him to learn. A huge lady from Arkansas approached me at the Great Outdoor Festival in Memphis and asked if it was okay for her dogs to watch our demonstration.

"No problem," I replied. "Bring them along."

"I have them right here," she said, and lifted two tiny little pups from her cavernous coat pocket saying. "Y'all just listen up now."

I'd like to think that she was kidding but somehow I doubt it.

I saw a picture in a training manual recently that actually showed the handler having a tug of war with his young Lab. How conducive was that towards developing a soft-mouthed delivery?

Ultimately, perhaps you want your dog to hunt alongside others or back up a bird dog. If so, you need to ensure that he is comfortable and steady in the presence of other dogs. Encouraging him to run wild with the neighbor's dog while you chew the fat is not a good foundation. Playing chase with other dogs is a habit much easier to start than to stop.

A lady once came to me in tears saying that no one wanted to use her working Labrador as a stud dog.

"They don't like his short legs," she complained.

"He had short legs when you bought him," I replied. "No one has sawed them down."

"Yes, I know, but I always wanted him to be a stud dog."

This was clearly a case where her ultimate goal was in total conflict with her selection.

So many dogs fail to reach their true potential and owners rarely have the dog they really want. They may have a dog they love, but not the one they visualized. A retriever is a huge commitment in time, emotion, cost, and travel, but with over 20,000 pups registered in the U.S. *every month*, there is absolutely no need for anyone to be disappointed.

Clarifying your objectives, choosing carefully, and following a sound progressive training program will fulfill all your dreams. You'll need self-discipline, patience, and a cooperative family, but the end result will be more than worth the effort.

Having a steady, obedient dog at your side that knows precisely when he is required to spring into action really isn't all that difficult. It's not magic; it's training.

Make a vow this instant to write down your goals, but be sensible. The lady with the short-legged Labrador was

CHAPTER ONE: SETTING YOUR OBJECTIVES

never going to make him into a stud dog, was she? You won't change a headstrong six-year-old Flatcoat that's never been steady into a docile, biddable gundog either, but you can improve his performance. You can certainly teach him not to break.

If you have a young pup of the right pedigree then the world is your oyster, and only you and your training stand between him and your "dream dog." The younger the dog the less it takes to change his habits, but even older dogs can learn.

Discourage bad habits at an early age.

One of my pals had a wonderful seven-year-old English springer spaniel with only one serious fault: he chased cattle. He could be working diligently flushing birds but the moment he drifted into the vicinity of cows, he terrorized them just for fun.

One day he was sent back on a long retrieve for a rabbit. The doe had disappeared down a burrow by the time he arrived, but he spotted cattle in the adjoining field and could not resist the temptation.

The cows all had calves and didn't take kindly to his aggressive behavior and joined forces to defend their young. One caught him a glancing head butt that sent him reeling, while the others moved in menacingly. He was outnumbered by at least forty-to-one and whichever way he tried to escape they had him surrounded. The cows held their huge heads down at ground level and even without horns, they looked fearsome. He tried barking but it didn't work; they just bellowed back at him. The more desperate he became to escape, the more aggressively they reacted.

He made a break for it but they immediately closed the circle, trapping him in the center. The ring grew ever smaller and by the time we chased them away, the dog was frantic and slavering with fear. That dog never took liberties with cattle ever again. So you see, it is possible to teach an old dog new tricks. Just ask any cow.

Some newly reformed behaviors are heavy maintenance and have to be re-taught periodically. A dog that has dropped birds at your feet for six years is not going to deliver smartly to hand for the rest of his life after one lesson. You are going to have to give him a regular refresher course.

The mind of a newborn pup is a totally blank sheet, but not for long. Just like a human baby, he will be learning good and bad habits each and every day. It's up to you to ensure that everything he does moves him closer to your ultimate objective.

Setting Goals
Talk to your family and decide what is a realistic goal for your dog. If the family can't resist petting him, handing out tidbits, and letting him jump around on the sofa, you have to lower your sights. If you can persuade them to follow your regime or, better still, leave him entirely to you, then you can aim higher.

Chapter One: Setting Your Objectives

Maybe you have to buy a "Max" for your family to romp around with while you keep your dog for the serious stuff? It could save a lot of arguments.

At a recent workshop I asked the participants to state at the outset the type of dog they ultimately wanted their pup to be. The answers were as follows:

"A serious Hunt Test dog"
"A top class duck dog"
"A companion/ retriever, competent but quiet"
"A good handling dog"
"A steady dog"
"Under control"
"Just an obedient dog"
"A good buddy"

Never buy a pup from any kennel that cannot show you the mother. By far, the biggest influence on your pup will come from mom.

Providing the lady who had aspirations for "a serious hunt test dog" had a pup with the right genes, and the guy who simply wanted "a good buddy" didn't have a pit bull, they all had a chance to achieve their objectives, and so have you.

Choosing the Right Dog for You
Prospective owners should think carefully about the sort of dog that suits their personality. If you are a big guy with a loud voice and a quick temper, a sensitive dog is not for you. On the other hand, it could be perfect for a lady owner with a more gentle approach. Tough, hard-going dogs need firm handling and unless you are prepared for the challenge they present, you may find the effort exhausting.

Like father, like son.

Chapter One: Setting Your Objectives

An examination of the pedigree of most dogs will give you an indication of what to expect. A stud dog that has a history of siring hard-headed, high-octane progeny is unlikely to suddenly lose that trait. Females that have produced quiet, biddable offspring will in all likelihood continue to do so. There are no guarantees, but you have to play the odds.

If you decide to buy a started or finished dog then you can choose with more certainty. You will know exactly what kind of dog you have from day one. It's a low risk strategy and one I would highly recommend to a novice owner.

Never buy a pup from any kennel that cannot show you the mother. Take a careful look at her. Whatever traits she has will be passed on to her litter. Nervous females produce nervous pups. Mothers account for the majority of the genetic make-up of their offspring. If you can see both the sire and dam at work, then so much the better.

Most breeders of working retrievers won't use a stud dog unless they have seen him at work in the field. They want to assess his style and temperament to predict the outcome of a mating with their female. You should try and do the same.

If a tough, fast dog appeals to you, then you need a pup bred from such parentage. If, like me, you are prepared to sacrifice outright speed for a thoughtful, intelligent worker, then you need to see those traits displayed in its ancestry or at least in the sire and dam.

The mismatching of owners to dogs is probably one of the most common reasons for ongoing training problems. I had a very expensive black Lab pup bred champion-to-champion who was undoubtedly the smartest dog I ever trained. He was also the most challenging. Whilst he learned faster than any dog in the kennel, he wanted to test me out on a daily basis. He would refuse the stop whistle at a distance to see if I would respond or ignore a cast and wait for my reaction. After his first season, he genuinely believed he could do the job on his own and needed continuous reminders that he was only one part of the team. Despite his amazing intelligence, I was not sorry to see him go.

In contrast, I had a nervous young Lab that my wife named "Velcro" because nothing would move him from my side. Not even a retrieve. He was too scared to leave me, but once he gained confidence he was a joy to train. He had the attitude, "If you can show me what you want, I'll do it."

He took much longer to tutor due to his diffident nature, but there was a lot more bonding during the process. He came to trust me implicitly and I him. He never let me down and always gave me his best shot. He wasn't as fast or as stylish as my champion-to-champion dog, but he suited me far better. He's in Colorado now having a great life with his delighted new owner.

Choosing a Breed

Generally speaking, I have found goldens slower to train than Labs. They rarely display the same drive but have irresistible personalities. Goldens like to play as hard as they work. They are brilliant with children and I have yet to see one that wasn't attractive, so if you have the time and the inclination, maybe you should consider a golden.

CHAPTER ONE: SETTING YOUR OBJECTIVES

Flatcoats are the aristocrats of the retriever world and a law unto themselves. Owners who have come to terms with their idiosyncrasies are usually hooked for life. They are wonderful looking animals and incredibly loyal, but they mature much slower than other retriever breeds and need a lot of patience.

Chesapeakes are independent personalities and whatever they lack in pace they make up for in persistence. I know they have a bad rep for being territorial and aggressive, but I never met one I didn't like. They take time to get to know, but make great companions and have coats that don't shed all over the house.

There are many retriever breeds to choose from, including (clockwise from top left) the golden, Chesapeake Bay, flat-coated, and Labrador retrievers.

The choice is endless, but if you just want the best working dog available in the shortest period of time, nothing comes close to a Lab. They are extremely biddable, learn quickly, are great with kids, and have all the style and drive any hunter could want.

Male or Female?
Once you have determined the breed, it's time for some honest self-analysis. Would you really make a good partner for a tough, hard-going dog? Such an animal is likely to be difficult to hold and you will need to be nimble on your feet if you are going to keep one step ahead?

Do you want a female? Can you live with leaving her at home when she comes into season while your buddies' dogs get all the birds? Females are sometimes quicker to train but can also present more complicated medical and psychological problems. Are you prepared for a possible collapse in form as she goes into and out of season?

Males, on the other hand, are often more challenging, requiring regular reminders of their status. They don't always learn as fast as females but never suffer a sudden hormonal lapse during training.

All these questions are best asked *before* you commit to a pup rather than afterwards. It's much easier to work with a dog that suits your requirements and temperament.

Other Considerations
Do your homework: study those pedigrees and solicit the opinions of old timers who know the breed lines and have seen the dogs in action. They will be delighted to share their knowledge with you.

CHAPTER ONE: SETTING YOUR OBJECTIVES

If you do your homework and choose the right litter, just reach in and pick out any one of them.

I once had a bitch that was absolutely brilliant on bumpers but unmanageable when she moved onto the real thing. As soon as she experienced game she became impossible to handle and went completely off the whistle. Midge was a "hunting machine" who ignored any attempt to handle her once she was on bird scent.

I was cursing her obstinacy when an elderly dog man asked me about her breeding. I told him what I remembered.

"Not much of a surprise then," he replied. "Her grandmothers on both sides (sire and dam) were exactly the same. Great noses but difficult to handle."

In one sentence he told me what it had taken me twelve month's hard work to discover. Consider how much time and wasted effort you can save by "reading the pedigree."

Some dogs demand the stimulation of training on a daily basis while others become jaded by such a routine, preferring to work only two or three times per week. What sort of regime would suit you?

Many working dogs will not tolerate much petting; some prefer their own company when off duty. My oldest dog, Blue, is so keen on his work that he will follow anyone that smells of ducks or pheasants. If he detects you can lead him to birds then his attention is all yours. He doesn't have time for fooling around; if you have a gun, he wants to see action and you better be good. He's been on enough hunts to know the guys who can shoot. He's an expert on marksmanship and intolerant of failure.

He was watching the sky from a duck blind recently when one of the gunners slipped him a tidbit. Without breaking concentration, he took it in at one side of his mouth and spat it out the other. Blue lives to work; he's not big on socializing. He'll swim 400 yards across a freezing lake for a blind retrieve or track a crippled pheasant through brambles sharp enough to shred a grizzly. All he asks in return is a little privacy. On duty he's all business; back home he likes to lay under my desk undisturbed. That's the deal. Is this your kind of dog? If not, then you would want to avoid Blue's bloodlines and find pups from parents that demonstrate a more lighthearted approach to life.

When you have answered all these questions, you will be ready to select your pup. Let's say that you have determined that your priorities are to have an excellent working Labrador that is relaxed and biddable.

That decision alone eliminates litters from hard-headed, high-octane parents or sires and/or dams that

Chapter One: Setting Your Objectives

have been known to produce such progeny. Consult other owners; members of retriever clubs are particularly generous with their knowledge. They can shed light on various breeders and their dogs.

Remember that by far the biggest influence on your pup will come from its mother. Find a female that has a reputation for its excellent work and biddable nature and enquire if the owner intends to breed. If you can find a female that has already produced such litters then so much the better.

Once you have tracked down your breeder, checked out the mother, and paid your deposit, your work is almost done. Thousands of articles have been written on "choosing a puppy," which would have been better aimed at "selecting a litter."

If you have been honest with your self-assessment, done your homework, and found an appropriate litter, then just close your eyes and pick a pup. There is no test on earth that will enable you to work out which pup will mature into the best dog. So if you have been lucky enough to find the right litter but don't have first pick, relax… it matters not a jot.

If, however, you are asked to transfer onto another litter for any reason, then your enquiries should begin again. The secret to success is in finding the right parents.

Chapter Two
THE PACK MENTALITY

The Ducks Unlimited mascot retriever, Drake, enjoyed having the company of a fellow Brit at the Great Outdoor Festival in Memphis. We were taking a relaxing stroll between numerous demonstrations when a huge gentleman wearing frayed denim overalls and a long, unkempt, ginger beard stood directly in our path. Drake and I stared up, anticipating trouble of the "Y'all pokin' fun at me, boy?" variety.

To our complete amazement, the giant bent down, patted Drake on the head and said, "He's just a little guy in a doggie costume." Unfortunately, this is how our society now views all animals. It's what I call the "Disney Effect."

The "Disney Effect" decrees that all species have exactly the same value system as humans (anthropomorphism). Thankfully, this is not the case. Retrievers don't steal your gal, shop at Sacks, or wreck your car, but the concept persists. Should you be tempted to treat your dog in this manner, don't be surprised if he is unruly and stubborn. Although your beloved companion may need food, water, and shelter, there is one thing he craves above all others: leadership.

In the wild, any dog without the security of a leader will not last long. In a wolf pack, the leading pair determine where and when the group eats, sleeps, and hunts, always assuming the greatest danger themselves. Having a leader allows the rest of the pack to relax in the knowledge that a greater authority is taking care of business.

In the absence of a clear leader (Alpha), most dogs develop neurotic tendencies, sometimes assuming leadership themselves with undesirable consequences. Whether you and your pup live alone or with several other dogs and a busload of kids, your pup will regard you all as his "pack." It is imperative for him to know where he fits into the pecking order. As a young dog he will be prepared to be at the bottom, but don't be fooled. He'll soon be looking for opportunities to move on up.

Very few dogs, male or female, are natural leaders and feel uncomfortable with the burden of responsibility.

In the absence of a clear leader, most dogs develop neurotic tendencies, sometimes assuming leadership themselves with undesirable consequences.

Chapter Two: The Pack Mentality

Despite centuries of domestication, our environment — with its televisions, cars, fridges, etc. — is still totally alien to them, and a dog who finds no leadership in a world that he doesn't understand soon becomes a dog under stress.

As a kid I used to babysit my uncle Bill's dog whenever my uncle attended a soccer match. Over the years, he had a succession of mad dogs. Whenever I visited I would ring the doorbell, triggering a salvo of non-stop barking that could be heard three blocks away. After a life and death struggle, Uncle Bill would finally open the door and two huge front paws would immediately pin me to the wall. "Don't raise your voice," Uncle Bill would urge as I attempted to wriggle free.

Following instructions, I would sit motionless on the sofa trying to watch TV while the dog stared directly at my crotch slavering and growling. Uncle Bill would don his cap and scarf, light up the stub of an old cigarette, and assure me that his dog (usually a rottweiler or a German shepherd) would never hurt me "unless you upset him."

As soon as Uncle Bill left the house I would invariably discover that breathing and smiling seemed to upset him, and any attempt to change channels on the TV sent the dog berserk. I spent hours sitting like a block of concrete, too afraid to cough or sneeze in case it triggered a feeding frenzy. The one and only time Uncle Bill did leave his dog alone in the house he returned to find his dining table had become a dinner tray; the dog ate all four legs.

Every dog Uncle Bill ever owned turned out the same way regardless of its breed or pedigree. Later in life, he even had a killer Corgi.

"I'm the unluckiest person in the world with dogs," he'd complain. It never occurred to him that he was the common denominator in the development of all these neurotic animals, providing no leadership whatsoever.

From the day you take your pup home, he's learning about the "pack" and his place within it. Early on he'll have his paws full trying to work out what goes where and who does what, but as he develops he'll start probing to see where he stands. Blue, my oldest Lab, always has a showdown with any new dog joining the kennels. It's his way of ensuring they are aware of his superior status. After that, both he and the new recruit usually settle down without any problems.

If your dog finds no leader, you can be sure of trouble.

Your young dog will not rest until he has identified the pack leader. He may decide that it's you and he may not, but if he finds no leader at all you can be sure of trouble. If you are to be the dog's trainer, it is absolutely imperative that you establish your leadership credentials. To expect a young dog to take instruction from more than

Chapter Two: The Pack Mentality

one trainer is both confusing and unreasonable, so decide early on who is to be Vince Lombardi, then assert your authority.

Pack leadership is communicated in four distinct ways:

1. Returning: Whenever the leader returns after absence from the pack, he does not acknowledge the existence of the other members. Pack leader stands tall and aloof while lower ranking members fuss around him. When they have paid homage to his presence and settled down, he rejoins the pack and mingles freely within the group. This ritual is reaffirmation of his status and allows other members to relax in the knowledge that pack order and security has been restored.

If you want to establish yourself as your pup's natural leader, you must have the discipline to follow pack rules when you return home or release him from his kennel. It's okay for him to be excited, but you must totally ignore his attentions. Do not make eye contact or speak a single word. Offer him no

...keep totally still and ignore your dog if he starts jumping up...

feedback at all. If you have a large dog that jumps up, simply lift your knee into his chest to protect yourself, but do not touch or push him away with your hands. As he adjusts to this routine, you will find he quits this behavior. After he settles down, greet him in a quiet and calm manner. Keep your voice low and do nothing to excite him. I know this may mean a significant departure from the normal high octane, "Hey, buddy, how are ya?" routine, but trust me, your dog will understand.

2. Controlling the food supply: Watch any wildlife film on TV and you will observe that among carnivores the strongest always eat first. When a pride of lions pull down a wildebeest, the leader is on first sitting and the rest of the pride take their turn later. Wolf packs operate in the same way and all dogs understand this unbroken law.

...always eat before your dog...

CHAPTER TWO: THE PACK MENTALITY

Control of the food supply is a very powerful method of communication.

Therefore, if you want to speak to your dog in a way that he understands, always have a cracker, cookie, or anything easily digestible that you can eat in front of your dog before you feed him.

Make him sit some distance away on "stay" while you prepare his food. Before you put his dish down, let him see you pick up your cracker and eat, making it very obvious. Slowly put his dish down and tell him to "get it." Every once in a while, pick up his dish before he has finished eating and hold it away from him for a couple of minutes, then replace it and order him to "get it" again.

This is the clearest indication you can give of your superior status, the significance of which will not be lost on your dog.

3. Leading the way: Pack leader is always in charge of the hunt for food, water, and shelter. He alone decides where and when the pack moves. Where he goes, the rest follow. No one goes ahead of the leader without his permission. Wolf packs since the dawn of time have observed this simple rule.

Your dog will instinctively know this. His ancestors for thousands of years have followed the same principal. Use it, therefore, to establish your leadership credentials. Never allow him to go through doors, gates, or streams ahead of you

If I want my dog to go before me I tell him to "get on;" without this command, he knows he must follow. If I'm entering a barn or large area he simply walks at heel,

37

... Never let the dog go in front of you at gates, doors etc ...

but if we have to pass through a narrow doorway or climb over a fence or stream, he knows the rules — I go first. Very soon your dog will acknowledge the message you are sending him by deferring to you whenever he meets an obstruction.

4. **Defending the pack**: All leaders defend the territory of their pack. Other members may ultimately join the fray, but it is the leader who initiates all defensive action. It is he who assesses the perceived danger and decides on the strategy. Strangers moving onto a wolf pack's territory will be observed by the leader and may be attacked or ignored; it's his call and it's at precisely this time that a pack without a leader will panic.

When visitors arrive at your home, your pup will bark in his kennel or rush to the door if he is in the house.

Chapter Two: The Pack Mentality

This is his warning that strangers are on pack territory. Should you fail to establish your leadership, he will assume the role himself, jumping up at guests or barking continually at passers by. If tolerated, this will upgrade his status and downgrade yours.

I taught my house dogs a long time ago to go to their crate on command. When visitors arrive I say, "Kennel," and they hop into their crate. To my kennel dogs barking outside I call, "That's enough." Both these commands inform them that their involvement is no longer necessary. Once your pup realizes that you are his leader, he will gratefully accept his lesser responsibilities and learn to calm down.

If your retriever lives in the house, it may be necessary to ask visitors to completely ignore any attempt by your dog to gain attention until he learns to relax in their presence. Guests should never be encouraged to make a big fuss of a boisterous young dog. This only reinforces his unruly conduct.

Very few dogs are natural leaders and many find the burden of responsibility awesome, leading to neurotic or inappropriate behavior, e.g. barking, aggression, pulling on the lead, destructive chewing, etc. Communicating to your pup in a language that he understands will convince him of your leadership credentials and pave the way for a much happier relationship.

Be consistent at all times, don't change the rules and you will gain his utmost respect. Treat him like a "little guy in a doggie costume" and he'll be the one asking, "Y'all pokin' fun at me, boy?"

Chapter Three
EARLY DAYS

One of the first questions anyone with a new retriever pup asks is, "Can he live in the house?" The obvious answer, of course, is that he's perfectly capable of living anywhere, but kenneling him outside makes control of his upbringing so much easier. As a pup develops, it is vital that his experiences lead him towards his ultimate role. The habits that he will learn are the foundation stone upon which his future will be built. It's much easier to prevent inappropriate behavior developing than it is to correct it later.

Formal training cannot begin until your dog has developed some power of concentration, which usually occurs around six months of age. Until that time, he must be socialized with animals and people in a variety of situations. Let him travel in your vehicle with you, but never encourage a young dog less than twelve months old to jump in and out of your truck — it can seriously damage his joints. Pick him up and lower him down; there will be plenty of time for jumping later.

If your pup is nervous of your truck, start feeding him in the back each day until he is happy to go inside. Initially take him on short journeys, but never feed him beforehand as he's much more likely to be travelsick on a full stomach.

Take him to the mall and walk him around the parking lot where it's not too busy. Let him meet other people as they walk to and from their vehicles.

If he's reluctant to walk on the lead, place the leash on him and allow him to trail it around the yard while he plays. He will soon become adjusted to it. Never use a choker on a small pup; it is far too severe and completely unnecessary. Buy him a puppy collar and a lightweight lead — that's all you need at this stage. If you are right-handed, he needs to be at your left leg, so always have some treats in your left-hand pocket ready to comfort or encourage him. Do not keep them in your right-hand pocket as he will be continually drawn to the wrong side — a habit you will have to correct later.

The intelligent use of tidbits at this early stage can help him overcome a lot of hurdles and turn a negative experience into a positive one. As he moves into formal training, treats will be slowly phased out, but for now they serve a useful purpose. Try and choose a tidbit he really likes and save it for training so that it retains its power to motivate.

Training Sessions
Pups need an awful lot of sleep so excursions and mini training sessions should be kept short and frequent. Five minutes in the yard learning to walk on the lead with you while encouraging him into position with tidbits and a quick session teaching him to "sit" is all his little brain can retain. You can repeat this two or three times a day

Chapter Three: Early Days

but five minutes is the absolute maximum at any one period. His time with you must be the highlight of his day. He should come out of his kennel bounding with enthusiasm for each session.

Remember that puppies need lots of sleep and have short attention spans. Keep training sessions short.

This situation is much more difficult to engineer if your pup lives in the house where there is constant stimulation. He's much less likely to be bowled over by the prospect of a five-minute session with you in the yard when he's been playing with the kids all day. It's very hard work maintaining discipline if your pup lives in the house and much of your later training will be spent trying to iron out the bad habits he acquired when you weren't looking. If you really must have him indoors, then buy a crate to limit his freedom when you both need a break.

Early Lessons

Coming When Called: The first lesson any retriever needs to learn is recall. A dog that will not come back on command is a danger to itself. Make your pup aware that you have treats. Encourage him to run freely around the yard, then call his name followed by "Come." If he doesn't respond, wave the treats allowing him to pick up the

Teaching your puppy to relieve on command is a very useful trick.

scent. The moment he arrives by your side, tell him, "Good Boy/Girl" and give him a tidbit. Your dog will soon learn that sprinting back on hearing your command has very desirable consequences.

Relieving on Command: You must teach your dog to relieve himself on command, which is very useful when you are on the road together. Here's how to do it.

Watch him as he plays in the yard and the moment he stops for toilet duty call, "Hurry" repeatedly followed by "Good Boy." Do it every time. When he's ready for serious training, he will already know that "Hurry" is his cue to do whatever he has to do before he starts work. Relieving himself whilst retrieving is not a desirable trait in a trained gundog.

Early Retrieves: All new owners are eager to see their pup in action and a lot of damage can be done by too many

Chapter Three: Early Days

meaningless retrieves. It's the quickest way to teach your dog to be unsteady. Give him something soft to pick up (I use a pair of old socks) and pitch them a few yards away in the yard. A couple of retrieves is plenty. Once you have established that he has a strong retrieving instinct, nothing further can be achieved. If he runs away with the socks or puppy dummy DO NOT CHASE HIM — therein lies disaster. It can take months to convince him that running off with a bird is not the best game in town. Tug o' wars are to be avoided at all costs and any desire on his part to take objects from the mouth of another dog should be soundly discouraged.

Using Food in Training
Use feeding time to teach patience, a quality so important to his future behavior in the field or the duck blind. Make him sit and wait instead of rushing to his food bowl the moment you put it down. Initially, a few seconds will suffice, then extend the waiting time day by day in small increments until he will wait for a couple of minutes before you give the command, "Get it." If

Your puppy will instinctively like to retrieve things for you. While it's tempting to keep throwing the ball or stuffed toy, don't do it.

he whines while he is waiting, slap him immediately on his nose and say, "No," in a very gruff voice. Whimpering, whining, and barking are not traits you want to encourage in a gundog, so don't tolerate it.

Introducing the Gun
Feeding time is a great opportunity to have him associate gunfire with pleasure. Once he will sit and wait for his food, leave him 30 yards away from you and the food. Fire a blank from a .22 pistol, then call him to you to eat. Eventually he will be comfortable enough with the noise for you to move closer until he's finally at your side. You can then repeat the same process with your shotgun, providing you don't have excitable neighbors.

Early Hunting Training
Even at this early stage you can teach him to hunt on command. Hide some tidbits in the yard, preferably something with a strong scent like slices of hot dog sausage. Lead him to the general area and tell him, "Dead bird." Help him to succeed by encouraging him to stay in the vicinity and make sure he is downwind of the treats. The moment he strikes pay dirt, call "Good boy" to let him know that's what you want. This is a game he will really enjoy. Keep repeating "Dead Bird" until he finds the tidbit, then instantly change to "Good boy." Soon he will start hunting the moment he hears the command.

Other Dogs
Let him meet other dogs in a controlled environment where you can easily intervene. Greeting another dog in

CHAPTER THREE: EARLY DAYS

Even at an early age you can start teaching commands like "Dead bird."

the yard and having a couple of minutes play poses no problems, but outside in the park is a very different matter. What are you going to do if he refuses your recall? Worse still, what happens when he disappears over the horizon heading for the road? Once he learns he can ignore you and get away with it, your job as a trainer becomes a great deal tougher. These are situations you must avoid.

My great friend Mike Stewart and I were training some clients' dogs at Wildrose Kennels in Mississippi. Everything was fine until one of the assistants brought out Alice, a young black Lab. The moment he removed her leash, she bounded towards the other dogs, jumping up and barking. In no time our quiet training session became a noisy free-for-all with dogs running wild or jumping in the lake. The moment she was in the company of other dogs, Alice had the concentration span of a gnat.

Over the next couple of weeks, Mike kept her under strict control and slowly began to make some progress. Alice became more focused and actually started to absorb some of her training. By the time her lady owner arrived the following Sunday, we were all quite pleased with Alice's improvement.

"I can't believe she is doing so well," said her surprised owner. "She is usually extremely boisterous in company."

Mike and I were quietly congratulating ourselves when Alice's owner asked, "Is it alright if I stay until it's time for her to play with the other dogs?"

We were speechless, and like a brave Brit I skulked off quickly (I learned a long time ago that arguing with a woman is like going through swing doors on skis) and left Mike to explain that "playing with the other dogs" was the precise cause of Alice's wild behavior.

Handle your pup frequently so he is accustomed to human touch.

CHAPTER THREE: EARLY DAYS

General Tips
Your pup should regard this early time together as pure fun and therefore formal correction at this point is inadvisable. Communicate your approval with a high-pitched, "Good Boy/Girl." Some behaviors are to be discouraged from the start and a firm "No" is sufficient. Be consistent and your pup will soon learn what you expect of him. For serious breaches in the code of conduct, like aggression, lift him up by his scruff, just as his mother would have done, and shake him while growling, "No." Save your praise for situations where his efforts justify a big reward; this will make it more meaningful.

Handle your pup frequently, rolling him on his back and running your hands along his stomach. Stroke the inside of his hind legs reassuring him as you go. This will build up his confidence in you and enable you to examine him whenever necessary with the minimum of resistance.

It is not wise to allow retriever pups to run free outside the yard. Once they discover the joys of chasing squirrels, rabbits, birds, etc., it's a tough habit to break. A young pup can learn everything he needs to know walking at your side or playing with you in the yard. Running around the great outdoors can wait until later, when he's acquired some basic obedience.

Your aim is to give your puppy the opportunity to sample all aspects of life in a positive and controlled manner. He should have some idea of the standards you expect, and sit and recall on command. If you have done your job correctly, he will recognize you as his pack leader and not demand undue attention or display inappropriate behavior. He will be comfortable in most situations and have developed no serious bad habits.

Around five or six months of age you will notice him giving you "the eye." This is a term veteran British trainers use to describe the manner maturing dogs have of looking to their handler for guidance. It's the moment when their powers of concentration have developed sufficiently to commence serious retriever training.

Choosing a Started or Finished Dog
If you harbor ambitions to have your new dog alongside you in the field or duck blind in the coming season, then you should most definitely consider acquiring a started or finished dog. Rushing a young pup into action is the surest way to undo all his training, often with disastrous consequences.

At any good professional kennel the only difference between a started and finished dog is actual game experience. The finished dog should have had at least one full hunting season. In all other respects, the started dog should meet the same training standard as a finished dog. He may not handle at the same distance, but he should be steady to feather and shot; honor in silence; stop on the whistle; and hunt on command. He should cast left, right, and back, and deliver to hand without dropping. It's impossible to prepare a quality dog in much less than twelve months, so you should look very critically at any started dog less than a year old.

Good finished dogs will invariably be two-and-a-half years old and upwards. It takes time and game experience to hone the skills necessary to become the complete

Chapter Three: Early Days

A started or finished dog should be steady to feather and shot; honor in silence; stop on the whistle; and hunt on command. If you don't have the time or patience to teach these skills yourself, a started or finished dog is a good option.

retriever. He should be low maintenance as regards training and may, in fact, show you how the job can be done. A good finished dog is a joy to own and I have seen too many great relationships formed between new owners and older dogs not to recognize the value of experience.

If you are new to the retriever world, an experienced finished dog can ease you into the training of a new pup, demonstrating what is and is not possible. It can also take the pressure off a young dog when the hunting season comes around. There is far less temptation to overwork a youngster when you have an experienced campaigner standing by.

Unfortunately, there is no way to erase mistakes you may make in training a pup — if you mess up it will show. Older dogs are a lot more forgiving. If you commit the odd error here and there, it's not likely to fundamentally affect his behavior as it can with a puppy. Should you send your experienced Lab on a retrieve and some badly trained dog takes the bird from his mouth, he probably won't hold it against you, but with a young dog it can create all sorts of problems.

Unless you are fit enough to chase after a pup every time he challenges your authority, you should definitely consider a finished dog. It's hard work proving to a young dog that you are in command. So if you don't relish the prospect of a physical challenge, maybe you should buy a finished dog.

There are still lots of refinements you can make in training a mature retriever, but they don't involve anywhere near as much energy. All the finished dogs I send over to the U.S. have to learn new skills: decoy work, quartering, entering and leaving duck blinds, etc., and I have yet to see one fail. Teaching new routines is a lot easier with a good quality finished dog that has already experienced the training process.

Additionally, it's a lot quicker to house train an older dog than it is a pup. No matter how long they have lived in a kennel, dogs do not like to soil their own sleeping quarters. So if you want to make a house dog out of a kennel dog, buy him a crate to sleep in. He will invariably keep it clean. First thing in the morning, let him out in the yard to relieve himself. In the daytime, confine him to the kitchen to limit the number of "accidents" and hustle him outside the moment he looks as though he needs to pee. Pretty soon he will adjust to the new regime.

Older dogs are much less likely to be destructive around the home, but any dog can chew the furniture if they become anxious or agitated. My sage and dependable dog, Blue, once busted out of his aluminum dog box and ate my leather upholstery when a group of young kids tormented him in the truck. Don't leave a new recruit unattended in the house until you know he has completely settled or you may come home to find you need a new kitchen.

A good started dog can be great fun. You don't have to worry about his early training; it's all been taken care of. Providing you maintain discipline you can move straight on to the more interesting business of fieldwork. A word of warning however: His first season will be one of great temptation and needs to be handled carefully. The transition from bumpers to birds is a major step and should not be rushed.

Early Training
When she's at work, your dog should have her full attention on the job at hand, so before you commence a training session, tell her to "Hurry" and let her relieve herself. You don't want a working dog that is in the habit of taking a pee when she should be marking a fall. (It's considered a serious fault in a British Trial dog.)

Obviously, you will be anxious to get to the exciting retrieving stuff but this is precisely where serious problems begin. Imagine taking a gifted first year medical student and placing her in charge of an ER department. Some days she may do reasonably well, but eventually the complexity, pace, and responsibilities of the job will unhinge her. This is precisely what happens when young dogs do too much too soon.

Whenever I hear an owner tell me that his eight-month-old retriever can perform 200-yard triples, I know there is trouble ahead. I want to respond with, "Yes, but what will he be doing in two years time?" Unfortunately, I already know the answer. I have seen far too many smart young pups develop into unsteady, self-employed, head-strong adults not to be able to predict the outcome.

Teaching a well-bred retriever to bring back bumpers is kid's stuff. Training him to be steady and obedient under extreme temptation is not. If you are aiming for exemplary

Your aim is to make a steady dog for years to come, not just a high-performing one-year-old.

behavior, then the fundamental building blocks have to be firmly in place. Your dog must walk perfectly to heel, regardless of outside influences. She must sit silently while guns fire and dogs run around her. She should recall immediately when she hears the whistle. In short, her basic obedience must be bomb proof.

One of the major differences between British and American training is in the time scale. When ten-month-old American retrievers are running triples, British dogs are still going through basic obedience. Many top English Field Trial Champions do nothing but sit, stay, and walk to heel at fourteen months old. Believe me, compared to training your dog to be steady, retrieving is a walk in the park. Remember what it was like teaching your kids to tidy their room, be polite at the dinner table, and not scream at each other? Yet how much difficulty did you have training them to eat ice cream? It's the same scenario.

No one ever called me and said, "Vic, I have a well-bred retriever who is steady, obedient, walks to heel, doesn't whine or whimper, and recalls on command, only problem is he won't retrieve." It's never happened; not once.

Mostly, owners complain that while their dog can bring back the birds, their steadiness and obedience leaves a lot to be desired. Too many retrievers break, whine, or chase. Very few will stop reliably on the whistle at distance, or obey a recall when they fail to find a bird. Lets look at how we can correct this.

How Dogs Learn
Dogs are not big on verbal communication. Whatever you may think, your dog understands very little of what you

say. When my wife comes home to find her golden has dug up the new plants, she scolds him and he leaves the room sulking.

"Why are you wasting your breath on him?" I ask, knowing that Max has difficulty remembering what he did ten seconds ago.

"He knows what I'm talking about," she says, wagging her finger at him. But Max doesn't have the slightest idea. She could be swearing the Oath of Allegiance for all he cares. Max simply reads her body language, a skill in which all dogs excel, and he knows whatever she's saying is not good.

If you want to put this to the test, next time your dog misbehaves and annoys you, gesticulate in an irritated manner and shout, "I did not have sexual relations with that woman." You will see your dog cower just as if you had scolded him (that's if he's not laughing).

It must be stressed, however, that dogs are not easily fooled. Their ability to read your genuine mood is uncanny and feigning annoyance is a waste of time. Pretending to be firm and resolute just won't work. Somewhere in your dog's make-up is a built-in polygraph that's impossible to beat. It's been handed down from his ancestors and honed by thousands of years of sharp-eyed observation.

It's no good preaching one thing but practicing something else — it won't wash. If you determine that your dog can come into the kitchen but no other room, he'll know if you mean it. Older dogs can read your intentions before you know them yourself. Set out the rules, keep them simple, and be consistent at all times. Your dog will respect you for it.

Pictures

Pictures are very important to your dog. He gains much of his learning from the illustrations he sees before him. When my young dogs go training, they jump up into the truck while I stand on the right-hand side and hold the door open. I call each of them by name and give the command, "Inside." One by one they load up.

One time, for reasons I can't remember, I stood on the left-hand side of the truck and went through the same routine, but none of them moved. The command remained the same, but they were unsure until I realized that I had inadvertently changed the picture. I switched sides and they jumped in without hesitation. Associating a picture with a command helps their learning process enormously.

Raising your right hand when you give the command to "sit" creates a recognizable picture, and repetition helps them understand. Later, in the field, you will be creating different pictures to help them grasp more complicated concepts.

Pitch and Tone

Your dog interprets your tone of voice much better than he understands your words. If you growl at him in a deep voice and tell him "No," he will pick up the meaning much quicker. When you want to confirm that he is doing the right thing, say "Good boy" in a high-pitched voice. Dogs like this high tone and will work to hear you use it. Be consistent at all times. Don't suddenly change "No" to "Bad boy," or you will confuse him.

Recently I heard a handler say to his errant young dog: "Y'all ought to be ashamed of yerself. It ain't no good being sorry. Fer two pins I'd whip your ass."

Your dog hears the pitch and tone of your voice more than distinct words.

God knows what his dog was thinking? All he needed was a firm "No."

You will never hear your retriever laughing, but he knows what it means. Dogs haven't observed us for centuries without realizing that laughter indicates approval. So don't snigger at your dog's antics unless you want to encourage a repeat performance. Should you find your young pup has chewed your gun slip to ribbons, do not laugh; in fact, don't even smile. He'll take it as a clear sign of consent and the state may run out of gun slips before you can cure him.

Pleasure versus Displeasure

Dogs learn by the contrast of pleasure and displeasure caused by their own actions. A young pup that is rewarded with a slice of hotdog sausage for responding to the recall

CHAPTER THREE: EARLY DAYS

whistle will soon compare this to the scolding he receives when he ignores it.

Do not make a big fuss over your dog for doing nothing. Make him work for your approval. It's a powerful tool that you can use in training throughout his entire life. You want him to place a high value on your relationship and you can only do this by restricting your petting and praise to times when he has completed a difficult task. If you are constantly fussing him your approval will mean nothing. He will know that he can gain it any time without effort.

With a young pup, you need to lead him into doing the right thing. If you ask him to "sit," hold his head up with the leash so that he's naturally inclined to lower his bottom. The moment it touches the floor, tell him "Good boy" in a high-pitched voice.

As he matures and moves into formal training, he must be made to do the right thing and experience displeasure if he chooses to disobey. (We will talk about praise and pressure later in the chapter.)

Be careful not to inadvertently reward or re-enforce "inappropriate behavior." If your pup runs off with your slipper, do not make the mistake of chasing after him. It will only show him how much pleasure is to be had by running away with a retrieved object. Later on, it could be a duck.

Repetition
You may be able to absorb something new after only one practice, but dogs do not. Unless it's some negative action learned as a consequence of a traumatic experi-

ence, dogs need many repetitions to grasp a new concept. They are also very geographic in their learning (their surroundings form part of the "picture"). Just because your dog will stop on the whistle at his regular training ground does not mean he will do so anywhere else. I wish I had a dollar for every surprised owner who told me, "He always does it at home."

That's why retriever training is so time consuming. It's not because of the duration of each session; it's due to the number of repetitions required in so many different locations. You may think that your dog knows when you hold your right hand out and say "over" he should go right, but that's not how he reads it.

From his standpoint he sees you holding out your right hand against the background of a white fence. When you move to new ground the picture changes. He now sees you, right arm extended, framed by a hillside. What's that supposed to mean to him? Perhaps at the next location, when you extend your right arm you will be standing in front of a tree creating yet another new picture. After many repetitions in many locations, he will finally work out that the one consistent communication is the extension of your right hand and the command "over." Then, and only then, will he truly understand.

Praise and Pressure
There are a number of "obedience trainers" who are convinced a dog can be taught anything by using only positive reinforcement. To someone like me who tends to form emotional attachments to his dogs, it's an attractive theory. As a result, I have traveled thousands of miles try-

CHAPTER THREE: EARLY DAYS

ing to find a field trial champion retriever that has been trained by such methods, but have sadly failed.

I have read repeatedly every word written by Monty Roberts about wild mustangs and his method for "join up." I don't think he's a fake; I believe he has genuinely unearthed a way to communicate with horses to achieve a specific result, and for that the equine world should be truly grateful.

Make sure you praise — or pressure — your dog when he understands its meaning.

Similarly, I know that if all you require is a well-behaved dog, establishing your leadership credentials, as previously discussed, is the only training required. However, should you aspire to own a serious working retriever, simply communicating your superior status is not enough. It certainly lays the foundation for learning, but that's all.

Years ago, retrievers, like horses, were "broken" rather than trained. Young dogs were initially encouraged to free hunt, chase game, and break in the mistaken belief that it was the only way to develop drive. After charging around unrestrained for the first twelve to eighteen months of their lives, these unfortunate animals were subsequently beaten senseless in a brutal attempt to curtail some of their acquired behaviors.

The idea was to eradicate any unsuitable conduct through severe punishment, leaving only the desired traits of a "trained" retriever. In practice, many dogs became so confused and terrified that they crawled along on their bellies, afraid to leave their master's side, while others learned to withstand the harsh treatment and continued to run wild.

Thankfully, such flawed theories are long gone and modern trainers are acutely aware of the importance of managing pups to prevent the development of undesirable traits. If young dogs are never put into a position where they can chase game, then there is no necessity to break the habit later. Trainers now accept that it is much easier (and kinder) to prevent inappropriate behavior than to cure it.

Guiding the development of working retrievers is now carried out almost entirely by praise and pressure, the amount and variety of both being determined by the age, experience, and temperament of the dog. A quiet, sensitive, young female will require lots of praise to encourage her to learn with very little applied pressure, while a boisterous, confident male may need exactly the opposite.

Praise can take the form of a high pitched, "Good Boy/Girl," light petting, or a small treat, while pressure can be exerted by a gruff voice, a shake, or a smack on the nose. As your dog begins to understand your commands, the amount of praise should diminish while the pressure

Chapter Three: Early Days

applied for willful disobedience increases. Save your praise for times of encouragement and real effort, not for simply responding to the obvious.

Blue and I were picking up (collecting the birds shot on a hunt) for a couple of well-healed country gentlemen who were shooting on the Scottish grouse moors last year. There were eight other gunners stretched out across the horizon, all excellent shots, while our two aristocratic gents were bringing down nothing but cripples.

Blue sitting pretty.

Time after time I had to send Blue out in hot pursuit. The temperature was in the eighties but Blue stuck to his job without losing a bird.

A few stragglers were still passing overhead when one of our gunners left his allotted position and came over.

"That's jolly fine dog work," he announced in a cultured voice, indicative of privilege and breeding. "Who's a clever boy then?" And he sat down on the heather to fuss Blue. It was a mistake. I should have warned him, but I didn't have time. Instead of pricking his ears and wagging his tail in subservient gratitude, Blue cleared his throat and spat a mouthful of wet feathers directly into the gentleman's face.

Blue has spent a lifetime retrieving game. Praising him for a job he's done a thousand times was meaningless. Later on, when we encountered a narrow wooden bridge across a noisy, fast-flowing river, Blue needed lots of encouragement. As he nervously made it to the other side, he wagged his tail like a puppy in response to my "Good boy." That was an appropriate use of praise.

Pressure is applied in the opposite manner. The more certain your dog is of the command, the greater the price for disobedience. Never, under any circumstances, apply pressure for any reason other than willful disobedience to a known command. If you have any doubt about your

Eventually, you need your dog to be able to behave in a group such as this one.

Chapter Three: Early Days

dog's understanding of your instructions, give him the benefit of the doubt.

Losing your temper and lashing out at your dog is disastrous. At best, it will screw up the drill you are working on; at worst, it will create a psychological black spot from which your dog may never recover, at least not under your tutelage.

The amount of pressure you apply must relate directly to the willfulness of the refusal. Were I to ask Blue to "stay" and he chose to wander off, he would expect big trouble. I would have no doubt that he understood the command and had made a conscious decision to disobey. He knows I would drag him by his scruff back to the exact spot where I told him to stay and shake him until his teeth rattled. Blue's been with me a long time; he knows the score.

On the other hand, should one of my young dogs make the mistake of going left on a right-hand cast, it would probably be due to uncertainty or lack of confidence. I would communicate this error with a simple, "No," and show him again what was required. Undue pressure in these circumstances would serve only to confuse him.

Some dogs that appear sensitive have simply learned effective avoidance techniques. If your dog is normally confident in company and comfortable with his environment but jumps up, bites the lead, lies down, or paws you the moment training commences, you can be sure you have a draft dodger.

Harris is a handsome male Labrador that came down to me from Scotland. When he first arrived, he crawled along on his belly, so I treated him with kid gloves. When he refused my command to "stay," I'd go after him and he would press himself flat against the floor looking terrified, so I kept the pressure right off.

After two months of training, he was still fooling around on simple drills and I began to wise up. When I was absolutely certain he knew what I was asking him to do, I applied more pressure and ignored his attempts to play dead. When he refused to walk quietly to heel as he had been taught, I grabbed him roughly and dragged him to the correct position shouting "heel." In no time at all he began to change his antics and to date is shaping up to be an excellent working retriever. Harris had adopted a very effective avoidance strategy to get him off the hook whenever he misbehaved.

Clear, concise instruction must be the order of the day, accompanied by praise when encouragement is required and appropriate pressure should the need arise. If you find yourself chasing around, shouting and waving your arms as your dog runs amok, *you* have mismanaged the session. All training should be conducted in an atmosphere of calm deliberation, and organized so that you retain control at all times. Giving a young pup a retrieve where there are other dogs playing close by is asking for trouble. You already know that he is likely to run off and ignore your recall, so don't do it. A few minutes planning before you begin will save your training session from becoming a shambles.

There is no set formula in retriever training; every dog is different and must be treated accordingly. I have a little yellow female in my kennel at the moment that has been poorly socialized. Despite being fourteen-months old, she is afraid of strangers and unsure of herself in unfamiliar surroundings. She needs lots of praise and encouragement to help her over these psychological hurdles. Pressure at this stage would be totally inappropriate. Later on, when she gains confidence, she will undoubtedly test me out and I will have to apply some low-level pressure to let her know who is in charge.

It's in the Timing
If praise and pressure are to mean anything to your dog, timing is absolutely critical. You must communicate immediately when the dog makes the right or wrong action.

Timing is crucial when you praise or pressure your pup.

It's no good yelling, "No," five minutes after he's eaten the steak off the table; he needs to hear it the moment he jumps up. Similarly, if you are recalling your pup, say "Good boy" as soon as he takes his first steps towards you.

Just as your dog is watching your body language, you must observe his. In training, he should be holding his tail low to indicate his willingness to follow your instructions. If he's running around waving his tail high like Old Glory, it's a sure indication that he thinks he's in charge.

When you reprimand him, watch his reaction. If his tail does not drop, you are making no impact on him at all. Conversely, if your dog is crawling along on his belly, you need to lift his confidence and lay off the pressure.

Equipment

Before we move into our first formal training session, a word about equipment. You would be amazed how little British trainers spend in this area. A British Acme numbered whistle that doesn't deafen everyone within earshot, a rope leash, half a dozen bumpers in a canvas game bag, some tennis balls, a starting pistol, an old shotgun, and that's it! I know American stores love to sell expensive leads adorned with enough chains and snaps to hog-tie an elephant, but for our training purposes, these are unnecessary. (You will find out why later. . . honest.) Just buy yourself a simple rope leash and leave Tarzan to train the elephants.

If you really want to splurge a year's salary on accessories, then go ahead, but believe me you don't need to. If owners spent as much time, money, and energy learning

Chapter Three: Early Days

how to handle their dogs as they do on purchasing equipment, the results would be spectacular.

The E-Collar Question

No new retriever-training manual would be complete without mention of the e-collar. (It would be like discussing the Clinton Administration without any reference to Monica).

No one in England uses an e-collar in training (well at least not officially). So in a determined effort to fully appreciate the benefits, I attended a five-day U.S. workshop before buying myself all the latest equipment.

I have to admit that I was impressed. An e-collar makes life so much easier for dog and trainer, and used correctly, it is very humane. Subsequently, I took several retrievers from pups to finished dogs with e-collar conditioning and training. Everything was fine until they started to become "collar smart." Slowly, they learned when the collar was on and when it wasn't, and they began to test me out.

I discovered that the respect shown to me simply evaporated once the collar was removed. Each dog I'd trained on the e-collar transformed itself into two dogs: the obedient one on the collar and the wilful one off the collar. Every dog became Dr Jekyll and Mr. Hyde. If you are a committed e-collar trainer and doubt my word, I suggest you hunt your dog without a collar throughout the next season and let me know the outcome.

In my humble opinion, no e-collar should ever be sold without a background check on the prospective owner. Timing, the e-collar's biggest asset, is also its greatest liability, and if you are inclined to lose your temper when frustrated, then e-collar training is definitely not for you.

Nothing upsets a confused young dog more than an unjustified correction. It can set back his training schedule for weeks and he can become so fearful of failure that he simply quits. Normally, when your dog makes a maddening error, by the time you get to him tempers have cooled and disaster avoided. Not so with the e-collar. Pressing the button takes but an ill-tempered nanosecond in which time your dog can be sent a message of such negativity that he never fully recovers. (Precisely the method used to snake-break dogs.)

I have no doubt that in the hands of a really knowledgeable trainer the e-collar is a valuable tool; unfortunately, there are a lot more e-collars out there than there are good trainers. The end result is that whilst most amateur trainers possess an e-collar, not too many own an obedient dog.

I was in the Midwest working some dogs recently when I saw a handler strap an e-collar onto his dog for the first time and encourage it to "go play." It galloped off as instructed and was immediately recalled while being simultaneously zapped with the e-collar. The dog stood frozen to the spot. The handler then increased the voltage, burning it repeatedly until the unfortunate animal bolted. As it hurtled across the field, the angry handler cranked the collar up to the max. His poor terrified dog flipped a complete somersault before rocketing into the woods.

In such circumstances, my normal affable disposition has been known to desert me and I too bolted... straight for the handler.

Chapter Three: Early Days

"What the hell are you doing?" I screamed, grabbing him in a hold worthy of Hulk Hogan.

"I'm gonna teach that crazy dog a lesson," he gasped.

"Is that so! And what lesson would that be?" I growled, pinning him to a nearby tree.

"I'm teaching him to come back when I call him."

"Brilliant, absolutely bloody brilliant!" I yelled, scarcely able to contain my anger. Had I been anywhere near a power line I would have been sorely tempted to hook him up "to teach him a lesson."

Now, just in case you are considering flinging this book in the trash muttering under your breath about smart-ass Brits telling Americans how to train their dogs, stick with me. Reading this is like taking antibiotics. You have to finish the course to feel better.

I genuinely find it hard to believe that anyone would think that shocking an unconditioned dog senseless would enable it to understand the appropriate response. It is no fault of the e-collar that such uneducated handlers exist, but should so many innocent dogs have to suffer?

In England, when a young dog lacks interest, drive, or natural ability, it is almost always given away as a pet, but trainers in the U.S. commonly use the e-collar to coerce the animal into compliance. Such methods do not a natural retriever make.

Unfortunately, these "flawed" dogs remain in the gene pool where they may be bred, further perpetuating their undesirable traits.

Unless you are a serious AKC field trial competitor, I see no reason why you need to use the e-collar. The best HRC dog I ever saw — 4xGRHRCH UH Mac's Southern

Belle Pepper MH — never wore an e-collar in her entire life. With a solid obedience foundation, patience, and a little ingenuity, it can be done.

For fixing faults on a hard-headed older dog, such as chasing or water refusals, an e-collar may be the kindest method, but you need to tread very carefully. If you are not prepared to spend three weeks collar-conditioning your dog (and yourself), you can create more problems than you solve. Zapping an unconditioned dog for switching birds on the water could encourage it not to pick any bird at all. Similarly, a dog nicked for chasing may decide that its route to salvation is to keep running, in the knowledge that he can turn off the collar by getting as far away from you as possible.

Mike Stewart and I were working the crowd at the Great Outdoor Festival when a handler told us that thanks to his (mis) use of the e-collar, he always knew where to find his dog when she ran off.

"And where would that be?" I asked, intrigued by his logic.

"She'll be right there in the Wal-Mart parking lot," he replied, proudly winking at his dog. "Yessir, ain't never let me down."

It hadn't occurred to him that Wal-Mart's parking lot was the precise location where the dog lost the signal and had therefore become a "safe place." His buddy later told me on the quiet that this was the only retriever his friend ever owned that didn't disappear for days, so I suppose having a "Wal-Mart" dog was something of an improvement.

Most amateurs do not have either the knowledge or the temperament to use the e-collar correctly and any pro

Chapter Three: Early Days

trainer who is unable to produce results without it is best avoided. Selecting the right pup with the right genes, ensuring it has a solid grounding in basic obedience, and most importantly, not rushing through the training program is, in my view, a much safer long term method.

See, that wasn't so bad was it?

Okay, we've already decided who is going to be Vince Lombardi; our dog is from sound, working stock; he's well socialized and looking at us with expectation. We've got a bag full of bumpers, a lead that won't break his neck, and a good whistle. Let's make a start.

Chapter Four

Learning the Fundamentals

By the time your pup reaches his first birthday, his manners should be impeccable. He should come when called; sit and stay regardless of outside influences; walk perfectly to heel at all times; ignore other dogs when working; only leave the truck or kennel when invited to do so; and never make a sound when on duty.

In puppy play you can teach your dog the meaning of "heel," "sit," "stay," and "recall" (come) with praise, tidbits, and little or no pressure. In the first few months of his life, we have to accept our pup has a very short concentration span, and therefore we are only trying to give him a basic understanding of what each of these commands mean.

You can encourage him to sit quite easily by holding the lead in your left hand and offering him a treat with your right held six inches above his head while saying "sit." It's natural for his rear to go down as his head goes up. As soon as he sits say, "Good boy" and give him his reward.

Asking him to "stay" is a little more difficult. Once he sits, you can encourage your puppy to stay by placing yourself between him and his food bowl and telling him to "stay." Make him sit still for a few seconds by placing him back on the same spot every time he tries to dodge past you with a firm "No." As soon as he stays on that spot for a few seconds, stand back and tell him to "Get it," and let him have his reward (dinner).

Teaching your puppy to recall (come) is easy. Let him play in the yard just before feeding time when he is hungry. Call his name, followed by several short pips on the whistle. Get down on your haunches and encourage him to you, and reward him with a tidbit the moment he arrives. He will soon learn the recall whistle means food.

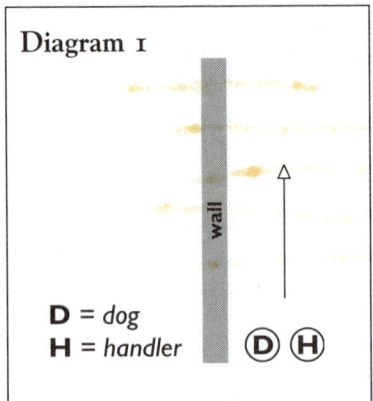

Diagram 1

D = dog
H = handler

Puppy heelwork should all be done walking along a wall (See Diagram 1) with your dog on your left side between you and the wall. (The wall cuts down his options and encourages him to walk close to your side). Hold a tidbit in front of his nose in your left hand. Tell him to "Heel" and the moment he wanders into the correct position, let him have a treat and confirm this is what you want with, "Good boy." You won't achieve great heelwork, but if you practice enough, he will instinctively want to be by your left side to get those tidbits.

Do not give him treats with your right hand or keep them in your right-hand pocket while doing heelwork; this will only encourage him to come around to the wrong side.

CHAPTER FOUR: LEARNING THE FUNDAMENTALS

The correct way to fit the leash.

Once he matures enough to absorb some formal instruction, it's time to set these puppy lessons in concrete as the basic foundation to all his future learning.

Heelwork
It's absolutely essential in training that you have your dog's full attention, particularly when he is at heel. He should be looking to you for instruction, not drifting behind or plowing ahead. Place the leash over your dog's head so that the neck loop slackens off when the lead is loose (ring up). If you put it on incorrectly, it will tighten when he pulls, but not release when he walks to heel (ring down). For what you are about to do, a choker chain is far too severe. It may be okay for an older dog that needs reminding of who's in charge, but for a pup, forget it.

Now tell your dog to "Heel" and walk smartly along,

but as soon as his attention wanders, about face, and snap him with the lead by giving it a sharp tug and releasing as you command, "Heel." When he catches up with you and assumes the correct position, repeat "Heel" followed by "Good boy," to confirm that this is what you want. Change direction every time you see his attention stray and snap him with the leash adding the word "Heel," and praise him when he's by your left side. Pretty soon, he will be watching where you are going rather than the other way around. It will become increasingly difficult to catch him out; when you turn he will go with you to avoid the snap. When he makes the turn without the need for you to snap him, say, "Good boy" so that he can compare your praise to the pressure of the snap. (Praise versus Pressure).

Do not prevent him from surging forward by holding him back on a tight leash. Keep the lead loose (it should have a big sag in the middle). If he decides to race ahead, let him. Before he realizes what you are up to, swing around in the opposite direction and snap the lead again and command, "Heel." Do not pull him round; it has no effect, just snap and release. He won't like it and will soon be keeping an eye on you at all times, which is exactly what you want. When you have him heeling correctly in a straight line, walk him in a figure of eight. Move clockwise, then counter-clockwise until he simply trots at your side whatever direction you take.

While he is learning correct heeling, do not take him on long walks. It's unfair to expect him to concentrate for prolonged periods. A five-minute walkabout teaching him to heel correctly is far better than a four-mile hike where he learns nothing.

CHAPTER FOUR: LEARNING THE FUNDAMENTALS

Now, with your dog on the lead at your left heel, walk quickly along a straight wall or fence (you'll see why in a minute). Stop suddenly and command him to "Sit." If he fails to respond, snap the lead above his head. Immediately when his rear touches the ground, say "Good boy."

Move off again, ordering him to "Heel." As you walk along the wall, stop suddenly and repeat the process. At first he will be inclined to flare out to the side, but the wall will prevent him and ensure he assumes correct position. Eventually he will understand that when you stop, he must sit down. Practice together until it becomes a reflex.

Many dogs never really understand what "Heel" means, but we can remedy this easily with a few sessions in the kitchen. Have your dog sit at your left side against the fridge or any flat surface (to prevent him flaring). Ask him to "Stay" while you move to another wall at 90

Using a fence to perfect heelwork.

79

degrees to him. Leave a narrow space between yourself and the wall and tell him to "Heel." If he understands, he will trot up beside you and squeeze into the space and sit at heel. If he doesn't, encourage him round by calling "Heel" and patting your left leg. The moment he moves into the correct position, call "Good boy." Repeat the process the following day and by your third or fourth session, you should be able to leave him sitting anywhere in the kitchen while you move to another spot. The moment you call "Heel," he should simply slot into the correct position. When he does this, you will know that he fully understands the meaning of "Heel."

Perfecting Heel
Later on, we must fine-tune his heelwork so that he has a precise location in which to walk, and that spot is with his right ear against your left leg. I carry a light garden cane upright against my right side ready to drop onto my dog's nose if he moves too far forward. I give him a sharp smack on the snout as I say, "Heel." You can also walk up and down a flight of steps with him at heel, where it will be very clear who is leading. If he surges in front, he will be taking the next step before you and when you correct him, it will be easier for him to understand what you want. A dog that genuinely understands "heel" will never go up or down a step before his handler.

Without an exact heeling position, dogs tend to creep forward a few inches until they steal half a length, and once your dog is allowed to walk or sit in front of you, it's so much easier for him to break.

When he walks perfectly to heel on the lead, wrap it

Chapter Four: Learning the Fundamentals

around his neck and have him walk along without you holding it. (He won't know.) Obviously, you can't do this with a chain big enough to anchor the USS Eisenhower. Sometimes I heel my dog on a leash made out of lightweight string so that when removed, he hardly knows the difference.

It's essential at this early stage for your dog to be uncertain whether you have the lead on him or not, so keep removing and replacing it as you walk along. This tactic will be even more important later when you are teaching your dog not to break.

Now that he knows exactly where he should be never allow him to stray out of position. There is absolutely no excuse for him to be anywhere else but at your side. If a bolt of lightening should suddenly strike and Elvis appears belting out a chorus of Jailhouse Rock, your dog should still remain quietly at heel.

If he continues to flair on "Sit," grab him roughly by the skin on his rump (the dog, not Elvis) and straighten him up as you say, "Heel." If you do this too gently, you'll be doing it for the rest of your life. So make it uncomfortable enough for your dog to decide that he would rather sit straight than be pulled into position.

I'm currently training a little female Lab named Gabby that has obviously been allowed to "flair" by her handler. Every time she sits I have to drag her into a square heeling position. Today, after a month of manhandling her into the correct position, she finally understood and came to sit perfectly by my left side. Now I know what Archimedes felt like when he ran naked down the street shouting, "Eureka!"

Recall

As a pup, your dog learned to come back to you (recall) for a reward. Now we can teach him to come back to your recall whistle without a reward. It didn't take him long to associate the whistle sound with hurtling back for a treat. Once you are convinced he understands this, he must respond. It's not advisable to move on to a trained retrieve without good recall.

As outside distractions increase, your dog will be tempted to ignore your recall whistle. If you accept this, he will learn that he only needs to come back to you when he decides to do so.

Take him out into the yard, drop a treat in long grass, and say "Dead bird." Let him hunt and find his reward. Do this a couple of times but on the third occasion, drop a stone instead of his treat. Say "Dead bird" and allow him to hunt for a few moments as you back off. When you are thirty yards away and while he is still searching, blow the recall whistle. The moment he looks up, crouch down and encourage him towards you while still blowing your whistle. If he moves in your direction, call "Good boy;" if he takes a few steps then turns back, growl "No."

If he totally ignores you, you must go to him and slip the lead over his head and jerk him towards you, snapping the lead as you do so while blowing the recall whistle. This needs to be done in such a way that it shows him very clearly what he should have done and be sufficiently uncomfortable for him not to want a repeat performance.

If you have done it correctly, the next time you try this he should respond to your whistle. If he does, do not think that your work on recall is complete. This is only

Chapter Four: Learning the Fundamentals

the start. Later you will find that bird scent, food, and other dogs make him deaf to your urgent recall command, but he must not be allowed to get away with it. Manage your recall training so that you are building up the distractions step by step. Don't progress from calling him back in the yard for a treat to recalling him off water; it's too big a step and you are inviting failure.

Try rubbing a cold bird on a pathway, then go get your dog and sit him downwind of the scent and facing you. Recall him to you and make sure that he ignores the temptation to investigate the scent behind him. Next recall him upwind over the very patch of grass you scented (See Diagram 2).

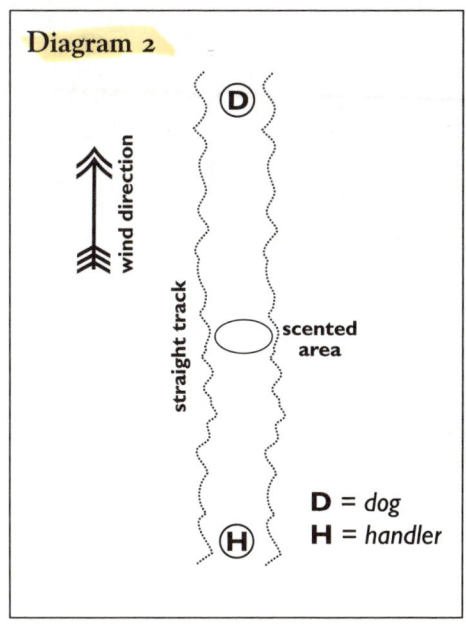

Finally allow him to examine the scented area and after a couple of minutes, recall him to you. If he ignores you, then it's out with the lead and another uncomfortable trip across the yard as you yank him towards you blowing the recall.

You can see how much more difficult it would be to do this in a large open area where your dog can run off and evade you. Plan each session carefully in advance and try to identify where things may go wrong. If the family is preparing a barbecue, it may not be a good idea to train in

Teaching your dogs to "Stay" in the kennel or truck until called out by name is a useful way to reinforce the "Stay" command daily.

the yard. Rolling around the grass with your hands wrapped around your dog's throat shouting "Gimme that steak" is not really conducive to the learning process.

As your dog understands that he must obey your recall continue the drill in a variety of locations and situations until he responds instantly wherever he is and whatever he is doing.

Stay

You may have taught your puppy to sit but young dogs do not like to "stay," particularly when they see you moving away (it's a security thing). The easiest way to teach "Stay" is with your pup sat in front of you on the lead. With your left hand, hold the lead a foot above his head; now hold up the palm of your right hand and command him to "Stay." This gives him a verbal command and a

Chapter Four: Learning the Fundamentals

picture. It is the same picture he will see later when he is working in the field and you want him to stop.

Keep hold of his lead with your left hand and back away as far as you can, telling him to "stay." If he attempts to move, growl "No" and place him back on the exact spot. Wait until he stays for a few seconds then return to him and reward him with a, "Good boy." Do not fuss him, as this will only excite him and encourage him to jump around.

Repeat this until he can do it without the need for you holding on to the lead. Now wrap the lead around his neck several times, tuck it in, and back away in the same manner. Over several days you should be able to move 20 to 30 yards away, but never turn your back on him. He is still in the learning process and you want to be able to communicate with a "No" immediately if he attempts to move.

At this early stage, do not call him to you from a stay — always return to his side. He's still trying to understand precisely what is required and calling him off a stay will serve only to confuse him.

You can now try it without the lead but be vigilant. Watch him all the time and do not give him any opportunity to break the stay. Walk around him in big circles — he won't like you going behind him and he will want to move. Don't worry if he turns around so long as he stays on the same spot. Slowly decrease the size of the circle until he will sit still while you walk all the way around him.

You can then command him to "Stay" while you climb over a fence or go through a gate. The moment he sees a barrier between the two of you, he will want to follow, but growl "No" to let him know he must stay. If he moves, drag him back to the original spot and start all over again.

85

If commanded to "Stay," your dog should stay put even when tempted not to!

When he will accept you walking around him and sit still while you climb over a fence or cross a stream, you can teach him to stay while you are out of sight. This is where you have to outwit him. Command him to stay, then hide behind a fence or door where you can observe him through a crack or small hole. You can be sure that he will move as soon as he's convinced that you have gone. But surprise him by reappearing and shouting "No," then drag him back to his original place.

You may have to do this many times before you can finally trust him to obey you, but these are battles you must win. During the War with Iraq, a popular joke in England was that it was being fought by a half a million American troops, two hundred thousand Brits, fifty Australians, three Portuguese, and the French surrendered "just in case." You cannot afford to surrender.

Your long-term relationship with your dog is not formed out in the field but in these "mini battles" taking place at close quarters where your pup will be observing just how resolute you are. If you are cleaning out kennels or doing yard work, utilize the time to practice steadying drills and leave your dog on stay while you cut the grass.

CHAPTER FOUR: LEARNING THE FUNDAMENTALS

Throw footballs or shoot hoops with the kids while your dog is made to sit and watch quietly. If he decides to lie down, so much the better. He is learning there are times when his involvement is not required.

Once you can guarantee his compliance to the stay command under any circumstances, you have the foundation of a steady retriever.

Lie Down

Here's a real attitude changing exercise. With the leash on your dog, tell him "lie down" and stand on his lead as you do so, with your foot about 18 inches from his neck. He will have no option but to go down, but he won't like it and will struggle to throw you off balance. You must keep your foot on the lead until he quits struggling and lies still. You can reassure him with your voice but keep him down. Believe me, this will be a trial of wills and if he wins, your authority won't be worth spit.

Repeat this several times, then forget it until later in the day. It's a very intensive drill so don't do it for more than five minutes at a time. After several days of such repetition, he will realize that if he lies down quickly when you say so, he can prevent you stamping on the leash and forcing him down.

Quite apart from setting the tone of the relationship, this is a very useful command to teach for whenever you have need to examine your dog.

Place

One of the most useful commands I learned from an obedience trainer is "Place." When I give my dog this instruc-

87

Use wooden pallets to teach the "Place" command.

tion, he runs to a rubber mat and lays down. You can use this to great effect both in the house and the duck blind.

When we have visitors at home, I just tell Blue "Place" and he grumbles off to lie on his mat where he can't take advantage of gullible guests.

I can take his rubber mat anywhere and tell him "Place" and he will find it and lie down. He understands that as long as he is on his place mat he's off duty.

You can easily teach your dog to do this by using a small wooden platform or pallet, which makes it easy for him to identify a clear boundary. It needs to be about three feet square and at least a couple of inches off the ground. Approach it from behind and with your dog at heel, walk up to the right-hand edge of the platform. To remain at heel, he will have no choice but to mount the pallet. As he does so, say "Place" and give him a treat. After a number of days repeating this, he will learn that he can obtain a treat by mounting the platform whenever you say, "Place."

Next, leave a treat on the platform and walk away with your dog, then turn him around, release him, and say "Place." He will go racing back to the pallet for his tidbit — as soon as he leaps on the platform and gobbles his treat, command "Lie Down." Walk quietly up to him and give him another tidbit for obeying the "lie down" command.

Eventually he will learn that "Place" means run to the platform and lie down. Now all you have to do is find a rubber mat to leave on top of the platform so that your dog associates the mat with his "place."

He will soon go wherever the mat is for his treat and you can eliminate the platform and finally phase out the tidbits, replacing them with a little praise.

Your rubber "place" mat can accompany you wherever you go. To your dog, it will always be his safe place, and to you, somewhere to "park" your dog when his services are not required.

Shuffling Forward

Most young dogs have the irritating habit of shuffling forward whenever you turn your back and leave them on stay. This is not good discipline, as they are simply learning to take liberties and must be taught that "Stay" means "Do not move."

The wooden platform referred to above is an excellent piece of equipment to prevent shuffling. It gives a precise location for your dog to "stay." The moment his paw moves off the platform, reprimand him with a firm, "No," and lightly praise him with, "Good boy" when he withdraws it back on to the platform.

Leave him sat on the platform while you go into the kitchen and eat a leisurely breakfast, but watch him through the window. The moment he attempts to move, growl at him until he sits still.

This is a great way to teach steadiness, but a lousy way to lose weight.

Silence is Golden — Eliminating Whining

In the final series of a recent British Field Trial I attended, the remaining handlers were asked to sit their dogs off lead for a duck drive. This involved a large number of mallard being "driven" off a pond in a nearby wood by the gamekeeper and his "beaters" (assistants employed to help flush game) and their spaniels. As the ducks took flight, the nearby guns opened fire and mallard rained from the sky.

The dog closest to me was almost struck by a falling bird that hit the ground and then waddled off down the entire line of dogs protesting like Daffy Duck. A golden shuffled uneasily, but was soon distracted by other birds thudding to earth. Handlers were forbidden to communicate with their dogs and stood rigidly by their sides with bated breath.

One young Lab in the center of the line shuffled forward three feet and was immediately disqualified. Near the end of the drive, there were dozens of ducks lying within thirty yards of the competitors, but despite the cacophony of noise still emanating from the woodland, all dogs remained silent.

CHAPTER FOUR: LEARNING THE FUNDAMENTALS

You want your dog to be patient and quiet while you are hunting — whining should absolutely not be tolerated.

Two weeks later I attended an AKC Field Trial where not one of the competing dogs was able to stay quiet. Some barked on being sent whilst others whined and whimpered in the blind. Handlers had to work furiously to heel their dogs to the line. In these events, such unruly behavior carries little penalty, but in a duck blind or upland hunt, it can ruin the day.

At a recent workshop I ran in Mississippi, a young handler arrived with a very handsome black Lab named Jake. The dog was only seven-months old but was already running long doubles and blinds. He had been trained entirely by his owner who had followed a prescribed schedule with great enthusiasm and dedication.

"He's picked up more than forty ducks already," said his proud owner, and I immediately anticipated problems. I didn't have to wait long. As we gathered with our dogs for the group discussion, our conversation was drowned out by Jake's continual whining. "He does it all the time in the blind," his owner confessed. "It drives me crazy." Jake was the only dog that broke when we sat our dogs in a circle and threw bumpers over them.

By the end of the afternoon session, Jake's owner was distraught. His dog, which had looked so impressive rocketing out for bumpers, was totally unable to withstand the pressure of inactivity. Time and time again he had to be reprimanded for his impatient whining.

"How can I keep him quiet?" He asked me in desperation.

I was reluctant to say, knowing that he would not welcome the answer.

Like all faults, whining has only three root causes: genetics, experience, and training. Let's examine each in turn.

Genetics: As we all know, there is no absolute guarantee that a pup sired by a champion will become a winner. The best dog I ever handled had a most unimpressive pedigree but it is not a formula I would recommend; the odds are far too long.

Generally speaking, if you need a guard dog it's better to acquire a rottweiler than a poodle. And if you want it to be aggressive, make sure it comes from a long line of biters. That way you will know it has the "right stuff."

You can be more precise by examining the pedigree for specific traits. Dogs that are quiet and steady tend to produce litters with those characteristics. Barkers are prone to produce barkers.

So before you buy your pup, make sure that you know the personality traits of its parents. That way, you will have some idea of what the future might hold. If mom and pop were both impatient whiners, you know what to expect.

Experience: Pups are taught very little by observing older dogs, but almost all of it is undesirable. They learn how to steal food, which is the best chair leg to chew, and where to have a pee, but never how to behave. When questioned, older, wiser dogs always take the fifth, denying any responsibility, but personally I don't trust them. They can be real sneaky.

One of the easiest habits for a young retriever to learn is whining. When a pup sees how older dogs, higher up the pack order, react to temptation, he soon learns to join in. It's a reflex reaction.

It is very rare to hear a dozen hungry dogs whining and barking for food while one sits it out in silence. It just doesn't happen. The anxiety of being left out is too great; he has to stake his claim.

Therefore, if you want to prevent your dog from making unnecessary noise, keep him away from dogs that do.

Also, try not to let your dog see or hear you working other dogs while he is left in the truck — you are inviting him to voice his objections. Park where he can't see or hear what you are doing. If he barks when you leave him, you may have to trick him by hiding close by, sneaking back, and surprising him with a reprimand.

Training: Incorrect early training is by far the biggest reason for persistent whining in older dogs. It has become common practice in America to start pups on marked retrieves from the get-go. Experienced and successful AKC Field Trial trainers may approve of this, as it carries

93

no penalty for them, but for the average handler it is the root of many problems.

If you want a quiet, steady, and obedient retriever it must first learn to be patient. For a well-bred pup, the retrieving part of its education will be easy. Once you have established that your pup has the basic desire to retrieve, this part of his education can be put on the back burner while he learns self-discipline.

In Britain, where steadiness plays a major part in Field Trials, young dogs are taught to sit and stay for hours under increasing amounts of pressure. It is quite common for a trainer to leave his young dogs sat in the yard while he throws tennis balls from an upstairs window as a distraction.

They are taught to "wait" before jumping out of the truck or leaving the kennel, ignore other dogs while working, and to sit quietly in line while more experienced dogs are sent to retrieve. But most of all, they are kept guessing. It is anticipation that creates unsteadiness in young dogs and the

Teach your young dog to be steady around any distraction or temptation — like chickens!

Chapter Four: Learning the Fundamentals

longer they can be prevented from knowing the next move, the better. Keep your training routine fluid and rotate your regime regularly.

Formal training usually begins between four and six months of age, and any activity that allows pups to run out of control is to be avoided like the plague. Permitting young dogs extended periods of unsupervised free running is a sure way to unsteadiness. Should they discover the joys of chasing rabbits, squirrels, deer, etc., you will have a major problem to resolve.

As previously stated, by the time your pup reaches his first birthday, his manners should be impeccable. He should come when called; sit and stay regardless of outside influences; walk perfectly to heel at all times; ignore other dogs when working; only leave the truck or kennel when invited to do so; and never make a sound when on duty.

If you have achieved this, then you have created an excellent foundation on which to base your field training, but beware. Countless marked retrieves are the quickest way to undo all your hard work. Instead, drop a bumper in front of your dog and heel him away in the opposite direction. When you have walked some distance from the dummy, turn him around, make him wait a few seconds, then send him back. This way he will have the reward of a retrieve while still learning to be patient

As his confidence grows, you can increase the distance and turn the retrieve into a blind. If you are training in company, you can send him for the odd mark after making him wait while others retrieve before him.

Unless he has made a major breakthrough in training, avoid petting him at work — it will encourage unsteadiness and a confident dog will read it as a sign of weakness in you.

Move slowly around your dog and avoid exciting him by keeping your voice level down. It's impossible to have a quiet, steady dog if you are jumping around shouting and waving your arms. You will be surprised how calm your dog will become if you set the example.

A few years ago I had the pleasure of watching an amazing Labrador win a major competition. I remembered seeing the dog earlier in her career and although her fieldwork was exceptional, she was eliminated a couple of times for whimpering.

"How did you cure her?" I asked her owner/handler.

"I bored her to death," he replied.

I was intrigued, so I invited him back to the pub afterwards for a pint and a chat.

"She was obviously gifted," my man explained. "But far too eager. So I went hunting with her three days a week for an entire season without letting her have a single retrieve. Eventually, she got bored, switched off, and forgot about whining. When I reintroduced her to birds, she worked without a sound, but even now when we train I don't always let her have a retrieve."

How many owners have stylish and obedient retrievers at ten months old only to find that by the age of three their dog is completely self-employed? The reason for this change is insufficient grounding in early obedience and too many marked retrieves.

Many American Field Trial trainers have the opinion that such steady dogs lack drive (and for their type of competition it may be true), but for the average hunter it

CHAPTER FOUR: LEARNING THE FUNDAMENTALS

is not so. Unless you are hunting with SAM Missiles, the need to have your dog hurtle out 400 yards at the speed of sound will be rare. In my experience, quiet, steady dogs prove to be the best hunting companions, as they tend to use their noses and are less likely to overrun those missing cripples.

The wonderful thing about retrievers is their willingness to please, and providing that their early training is progressive and correct, there is no reason why anyone should have their hunt spoiled by a whining dog.

Finally, the noise and excitement of water work does put additional pressure to whine on honoring dogs and should only be undertaken when your dog is rock steady and silent while honoring on land.

At the end of an honoring session, do not start flinging bumpers around to reward your dog. Drop a dummy, walk him away, then turn, wait, and send him back. He will have the same fun but only a fraction of the excitement. You can do the same on water by throwing the bumper into the lake and retreating from the water's edge.

I know such inactivity will create serious withdrawal symptoms for handlers addicted to throwing countless bumpers, so I'm designing a T-shirt for these guys with the slogan: "Fun Bumpers... Just Say No."

Working On Weaknesses

One of the major differences I see between British and U.S. programs is the tendency of American trainers to concentrate on areas where their dogs naturally excel. Hence a hard-driving dog is given dozens of increasingly long, difficult retrieves and in fairness, many of these dogs

If you have a naturally hard-running dog, you'll have to work on short-distance retrieves to teach her to hunt close.

become super-retrievers, able to mark with the accuracy of a laser but hotter than a pistol. If you plan to run AKC field trials, stick with the program... if not, follow me.

Alex, my teenage assistant who helps run my kennel, loves driving my truck and on weekends, one of his jobs is to take it down to the gas station, check the tires, and fill the tank. first he has to jet wash the kennels, lay down fresh sawdust, clean out all the water buckets, and mow the grass. I don't have to remind him to take the truck; he never forgets, even when he's pushed for time. That's why I make sure it's last on his list. It's the one thing I don't need to check. Left to his own devices, he'd be the best truck driver in town and I'd be left with all the yard work.

Training your retriever to be an all-round performer is no different. You must work on his weaknesses. If he is a hard-driving dog, work on steadiness. If he is rock

CHAPTER FOUR: LEARNING THE FUNDAMENTALS

steady but lacks real enthusiasm, get him rushing out for lots of bumpers.

If you have a dog that hunts with his eyes, then you need to teach him to use his nose. Throw a tennis ball in heavy cover and tell him "Dead bird." Give him lots of praise immediately he finds one. Make sure all his marked retrieves fall into cover where he has to use his nose. Site hunters soon learn to employ their superior nose power once they experience the joy of success.

Conversely, naturally-gifted hunters love to explore every scent they encounter, so these dogs need to be worked on "site" retrieves where a minimum of hunting is necessary. Drop a bright white bumper where it can be clearly seen. Walk your dog fifty yards away, then turn him round and send him back. If he stops to investigate a scent on the way, holler "No." Force him back to the bumper with the aim of achieving a straight-there-and-back retrieve. Make sure that the majority of his marked retrieves are clearly visible until you are confident that he is using his eyes as much as his nose.

A nervous dog that shies away from strangers should be gently exposed to lots of different situations and introduced gradually to new experiences. Encourage friends to pet him. Have treats handy for visitors to offer so that he forms a pleasant association with greeting people. If he's nervous around other dogs, encourage your buddies to drop by with their dogs and introduce them to him in the kitchen where you can supervise proceedings. Make sure that your friend's dog has a friendly persona before you attempt this. If your anxious dog receives an aggressive response, it would be a serious set back.

Confident dogs that have been well socialized should be discouraged from greeting visitors and other dogs unless specifically invited to do so. The last thing you want is a retriever that prefers fooling around with other dogs to working. Once my Labs are confident and relaxed in company, I train them to completely ignore other dogs.

Some dogs love to run and will hurtle out 200 yards whenever they are sent, but what about those birds that disappear into cover thirty yards away? A hard-running dog will be way past the fall before it even registers. You have to work on these short retrieves to teach him that he may be required to hunt closer. I'm currently running a talented female Lab that has had so many long retrieves she doesn't even draw breath until she's past the 100-yard marker. Katie is absolutely brilliant at 200 yards plus, but yesterday she lost a cripple in heavy cover twenty yards away. It was a blind retrieve and by the time I stopped her and convinced her to come back to the fall, the bird was long gone.

In contrast, I have Atom who loses confidence the farther he goes from my side. He would really prefer to work within a fifty-yard radius, so I give him nothing but long retrieves. I have to teach him to range farther afield.

Some retrievers hate water re-entries and need to be encouraged, coaxed, and cajoled into completing them. These dogs need regular water work. Others, like my Scottish dog, Harris, love water and are happy to make a thousand re-entries. I like to give these dogs lots of land retrieves close to the water to teach them that diving into the lake at every opportunity is not always required.

I give all my dogs two minutes to "Go hurry" just before we commence training. If they have been in the truck a

Chapter Four: Learning the Fundamentals

long time, it allows them time to stretch, shake, and go to the bathroom. Some dogs are reluctant to move from my side and I try to loosen them up by encouraging them to follow an older, more confident dog. Others take advantage of the moment and run off into the distance at the speed of light. I never allow them to do it twice. Once I'm aware of their natural inclination to stray, I call them back as soon as they range beyond thirty yards. No confident retriever should ever be permitted to wander beyond this distance from its handler unless sent on a retrieve.

Encouraging your dog to roam at will is simply inviting trouble. If he is allowed to drift away when there is no action, imagine what will happen on a hunt when there's gunfire to excite him and birds to chase.

If you have an insecure dog reluctant to leave your side, you may want to loosen him up and build his confidence with some free running. To do this, you must ensure the ground on which you exercise him is devoid of game, rabbits, squirrels, etc. Only then is it safe to encourage him to run freely. You don't want to replace a confidence problem with a serious chasing habit. Just as soon as you know he has shed his worries about leaving your side, revert to the thirty-yard rule.

For a dog lacking in enthusiasm, I suspend all the rules, allowing him to break, even when the bumper's in mid air. I give him as many marked retrieves as necessary to build up his desire. A quiet corner of the local Wal-Mart parking lot is a brilliant place to do this. He can see the bumper wherever it lands. A dummy falling into cover has only half the temptation of one bouncing off the black top.

Once I know the dog will go bounding out every time, I reintroduce steadying drills into his training.

Teaching Patience

No enthusiastic retriever is naturally patient. As a trainer, you must work on this continuously. Starting with a young puppy, you can make him wait for his dinner by standing between him and his food bowl until he sits down for a few seconds before you tell him to "Get it."

As he develops, you can introduce a degree of patience into almost everything he does. My dogs have to sit quietly outside the kennels while I clean them out. They are never allowed to jump down from the truck until invited to do so by name. I don't want a bunch of wild dogs knocking me over as they jostle to be first out of the blocks, so I teach them to wait.

Max, Atom, Daz, Bud, Ben, and Blue wait their turn to be sent.

Chapter Four: Learning the Fundamentals

As soon as my young dogs are through their basic one-on-one training and have a degree of steadiness, I let them join my training group. This includes older dogs who are out for daily exercise, finished dogs that need a little polish, started dogs working on hand signals, and my youngsters.

Each dog has my undivided attention for twenty to thirty minutes while the others sit quietly and wait their turn. This is excellent for developing patience but can be hard work for me when one or two of the young dogs start moving around. In this instance, I tell the dog I'm working to "Stay" while I return to the group and deal with the insurrection.

Usually, it's a young dog who thinks he can break the rules, but I drag him back to his place and insist that he stops there. No matter how many time he moves, I always put him back on the same spot. Usually I mark the exact place where I left the group with a stick so that I know if they have been shuffling forward. It's a habit the older dogs have when they think I'm not looking.

After a few altercations, most young dogs learn to be good citizens, content to sit with the group and wait their turn.

This week, things didn't go quite to plan. I've been trying to lose some weight but I'm constantly breaking my diet, so on Tuesday I made a foolproof plan. I was out for the day training and went without breakfast, taking only water and fruit for lunch. I deliberately left my cash at home so I wouldn't be tempted to buy pies or sandwiches later in the day.

During the mid morning training session, Blue went lame and I left him to rest up in the cab (Blue always travels up front). Four hours and six dogs later, I was dying on my feet. I had run out of steam completely. I was famished after burning up a month's supply of calories chasing young dogs up and down some of the steepest hills in England.

The low-calorie lunch now seemed like a really stupid idea. All I had was a banana, two pears, an apple, and bunch of grapes. That wasn't even going to touch the sides and I contemplated whether to munch the banana with the skin left on to help me make it through the rest of the day.

I dragged myself back to the truck and with hands shaking from fatigue, I flung open the door and discovered to my horror that Blue had devoured all the fruit — apple core, skins, pips, stems, everything. The only thing left was a soggy, brown paper bag.

Now I don't remember when I stopped screaming, but in my unbalanced state of mind, I genuinely considered eating Blue, and had he not been recently rolling in cow dung, I'd have done it.

Driving back, I dreamed up all sorts of gastric agonies Blue was going to suffer for helping himself to my spartan lunch, but he snored peacefully all the way home while I was racked with stomach cramp. Is that fair?

Delivery to Hand

It really isn't wise to start formal retrieving drills before your dog has learned the "hold" command. This is the point at which American trainers introduce "force fetch," often commencing with an ear pinch closely followed by pressure from the e-collar.

CHAPTER FOUR: LEARNING THE FUNDAMENTALS

To teach a dog to deliver to hand, you first must perfect the "Hold" command.

I can honestly say that I have never had to revert to force in order to teach a well-bred retriever to "hold." Most young pups will dash out for a pair of rolled up socks, but few will deliver them to hand, preferring to run off with their prize or drop it the moment something new takes their attention.

I start teaching the "hold" command soon after my dogs have finished teething (five to six months), usually in the kitchen where there are few distractions. Conventional wisdom states that using tidbits to teach the "hold" command encourages the dog to spit out the dummy in anticipation of his treat, and this is true —

until your pup learns that there is no tidbit forthcoming until *after* he delivers.

Let him know that you have tidbits, then throw a small bumper for him and encourage him back to you (it's easy in the kitchen when there's nowhere else to go). He will undoubtedly drop the dummy before he reaches you. Place it gently back in his mouth while repeating, "Hold it, good boy, hold it, good boy," and pull him towards you by his scruff, making sure that he doesn't drop it. Take the bumper and let him have his treat.

Do this for five minutes three times a day, and by the end of the week he will start to understand that only a completed delivery gains him a tidbit. You must be absolutely ruthless and give him his treat only after he delivers. As he begins to comprehend, encourage him to pick up the bumper himself when he drops it, instead of putting it back in his mouth. As soon as he brings it to you, give him his reward. Once he grasps the concept, he will gladly deliver to hand. Later you can be less predictable in dispensing the tidbits, eventually fazing them out altogether.

As soon as I'm convinced my dog fully understands the "hold" command, I make it a rule never to pick up anything he drops. He must collect any object lying on the ground that concerns him.

I always start the holding drill by flipping a bumper across the kitchen and telling my dog to "Fetch." Usually he will shoot across the floor and grab the bumper while I sit on a kitchen chair with my legs open. I try to encourage my pup to come back inside my legs while I hold a tidbit to my chest. If he has trouble understanding this, I

Chapter Four: Learning the Fundamentals

forget the bumper altogether and sit him at the far side of the kitchen, then blow the recall whistle. As soon as he comes and sits between my legs looking up at the tidbit, I let him have his reward. After several repetitions, my pup learns that assuming this position earns him a treat.

I teach all my dogs to deliver to the front, and by simply coming to me for a tidbit he's learning the correct position for a perfect delivery. I then go back to flipping the bumper and asking him to "Fetch." Initially he will drop the dummy in anticipation of the tidbit, but I place it back in his mouth as previously explained, only dispensing the tidbit when I have the bumper safely in my hand.

Once he sees how resolute I am, he starts picking up the dropped bumper himself and very soon learns that the quickest way to a tidbit is a straight out-and-back delivery. When this occurs, I start making him hold the bumper for longer periods before I take it from him. The moment he loosens his grip, I say "Hold it" and tap underneath his lower jaw, encouraging him to close it. I may then tell him to "Wait," with the bumper still in his mouth. I then move to the other side of the kitchen, always keeping my eye on my dog in case he loosens his hold. I then recall him to me and let him deliver again.

He now thoroughly understands the meaning of "Hold" and all that remains is for me to teach him when to release. I don't want my dog to drop a bird the moment he sees my hand coming towards him, so I tap the bumper with both hands and tell him to "Hold it." Sometimes this action causes confusion, but it doesn't take long to show him what is required.

This black Lab fully understands the "Hold" command.

Finally, I hold the bumper firmly and say, "Dead" (or you can say "Give"). It's important that my dog learns to open his mouth and turn his head away rather than me taking the bumpers from him. It's much harder for him to drop a bird if he needs me to hold it before he can release.

Once I'm convinced that he has mastered all aspects of delivery to hand, I phase out tidbits altogether and insist on compliance. Any time he drops a bumper, he will be made to pick it up and may have to walk to heel for 100 yards holding it in his mouth before I take it from him.

Older dogs that know the "Hold" command but have been allowed to drop require a different approach. Tidbits are a waste of time for these dogs. All retrieving should be suspended while the "Hold" command is reinforced.

Chapter Four: Learning the Fundamentals

Place the bumper in the dog's mouth and command him to "Hold it." Without taking your eyes from him, walk around him in a circle. The moment he attempts to drop it, go back to him and smack him beneath his lower jaw with a firm, "No. . . hold it." When he complies, stroke his chest and say, "Good boy." This will communicate to him what is required.

As soon as he will reliably hold it while you walk round him, command him to "Heel" and have him walk along side you holding the bumper. Then tell him to "Wait," walk twenty yards away, and recall him. If he looks like he may drop it, shout "Hold it." Don't take the bumper, but ask him to "Wait" again while you walk away and repeat the drill. Finally, tap the bumper with both hands while he holds it before taking it from him.

If you have a really stubborn character who has a deep-seeded habit of spitting out bumpers, switch to a tennis ball. This change is sometimes the key to breaking the practice; later you can reintroduce dummies.

Be determined; with an older more experienced dog who genuinely knows the hold command but refuses to obey, it may come down to a war of attrition.

Chapter Five
FORMAL RETRIEVING

Obviously, you want to teach your dog to retrieve, but in doing so you do not want to make him unsteady. It is countless marked retrieves that will cause him to break and whine. When your dog genuinely understands the "Hold" command, we can begin formal retrieving.

Singles
Walk him at heel along a wall or fence and let him see you drop a bumper. Turn around and walk away directly along the fence line. When you are twenty yards from the bumper, turn to face it and tell him to "Sit."

After he has settled, send him for the bumper by pointing with your left hand above his head and calling his name followed by "Get back." If he has forgotten about the dummy and continues to sit rock steady, toss another bumper ten yards in front of him, turn around on the spot, then send him back immediately. As soon as he picks the dummy, blow the recall whistle and keep blowing until he delivers it to you.

Once he has the idea and is running straight out and back, you can gradually extend the distance. The impor-

Here I am teaching Daz to retrieve with the command "Get back." Doing this drill along a fence or wall will keep your dog moving in a straight line.

tant factors in this drill are:
- A fence or wall to encourage him to run in a straight line.
- Short grass so that your dog can see the bumper clearly from the moment you send him.
- No distractions. (Don't try it around people and/or other dogs).

As he grows in confidence, you can drop the dummy and walk him away over streams and ditches before sending him back. This will enable him to understand that he may have to traverse such obstacles in his working life.

It helps to find a convenient landmark (like a tree), drop your bumper, walk away, and send him back from an appropriate distance.

The familiar sight will help him to go straight to the bumper instead of over-running it or hunting short. You are still looking for a straight out-and-back retrieve and anything that assists this objective is to be welcomed.

Doubles
Once he has this down, you can start him on doubles. Go back to the beginning, but this time throw TWO bumpers, spacing them at least ten yards apart to avoid tempting him to switch.

Don't walk more than twenty yards away. You may be surprised to find that after he has retrieved the first one he refuses to go again. If that's the case, make the process simpler and the time delay shorter. When he has the idea, you can extend the distance again. Pretty soon he'll be executing a double just as easily as a single.

When he is confident and knows the routine, you will find him wanting to break as soon as you turn him around, so here's what to do. As you walk away from the dropped bumpers, spin round a couple of times en route so that he never knows when you intend to send him.

Occasionally, line him up for a retrieve but instead of calling his name, cough, and wave your arms around. If he breaks nail him with a firm, "No." If he refuses to stop and beats you to the bumper, next time leave a rock to prevent him getting a reward. You want him to go when he is told to do so and not before.

If you discipline yourself to progress at a pace your dog can absorb, you will have a retriever that will work doubles or singles over any terrain at any time under perfect control.

Switching & Shopping

Switching bumpers, or "shopping" as my hunt test buddies refer to it, is highly undesirable. The frustration of watching your dog swimming around in the water switching from one bird to another is unbearable, especially if more ducks are on the way in. Like many other faults, it's a habit much easier to prevent than cure.

Start in the kitchen by tossing a couple of bumpers on the floor six feet apart. Tell your dog to "Fetch" and as soon as he picks the first bumper, really encourage him to bring it straight to you. If he tries to switch, yell "No" and growl at him.

He will soon get the idea and with you standing no more than a few feet away, you can manipulate the situation so that he has no choice but to comply. Once he understands, move into the yard and repeat the process, keeping the distance between you and the bumpers the same as it was in the kitchen.

If there's no problem, start extending the distance. It's a very easy concept to teach and young dogs soon get the hang of it. Older dogs that have sinned take more time and effort, but the principle is exactly the same.

Once you have your dog dashing out for one bumper and ignoring the second, you can introduce a third and fourth. As soon as he picks the first bumper, recall him. If he even looks at any of the others, yell "No!" and growl at him. As soon as he starts back towards you, call "Good boy." This will confirm what is required.

When he really understands the concept you can introduce distractions, like throwing a bumper behind you as he gallops back with his retrieve. If he looks as though he's going to go straight past you, step in his path and tell him, "No."

Later you can toss a bumper over your dog's head when he's on his way back. Finally, when he realizes that he must only retrieve the bumper he's sent for, you can hurl a diversion while he is on his outrun, but don't try this until he's 100 percent on all the other diversion drills.

Next, start on cold game but go back a good few stages, as the temptation of birds will prove far greater than a couple of old bumpers.

Water Retrieves

Once he has mastered all these distractions and diversions on land, you can start teaching him on water. (Of course, he should first be introduced to water and able to swim; see page 121 and additional information in Chapter 8.) Begin in the shallows by the shoreline and do exactly as you did in the kitchen, moving up slowly through all the stages.

When you first start throwing diversions on water, you can use rocks. If he is on his way back with a bumper and you throw a rock as a distraction, he will find it very difficult to swap (unless he's wearing a diving suit). Make him ignore the splash and come straight back with the dummy.

Having gone through the process on dry land, it won't take him long to work out what you want in the water. If he shows any sign of shopping, go back a few stages until you can exercise enough control to ensure he makes the correct choice.

Do not start launching dozens of bumpers into the middle of the lake as soon as you think he has grasped the

Don't toss bumpers into the middle of the lake until your dog has mastered retrieving in the shallows.

concept. It has to be ingrained as a habit before you can put that much temptation in his path. Build up to it gradually and don't chance your luck until he's 100 percent reliable in the shallows where you have a chance to intervene.

Field Trial dogs brought up on this kind of regime never think of switching birds. It's a habit they are never allowed to develop. Make sure your dog doesn't either.

Steadying

If your young dog shows little interest in retrieving, you must build up his desire by encouraging him to rush out unchecked for fun bumpers. Very few well-bred working retrievers require much of this stimulation.

Show/Breed dogs are often reluctant retrievers, and although they can be taught to fulfill a role, it is a long and laborious process. Forcing a dog through months of training for a job in which he has little natural inclination is both unrewarding and unnecessary. With so many well-bred working pups available, it makes little sense to persevere with a dog clearly unsuited to the task. My advice to

Chapter Five: Formal Retrieving

any owner in this situation is to accept your dog's limitations, make him the family pet, and find a more suitable working partner.

I find it strange that so many new owners spend as little as $200 on a pup of dubious breeding, then pay twice as much for an e-collar to make it perform. Buying a pup more suitable for the job would produce far better results. Once your dog will dash out with enthusiasm for a bumper, you can begin the steadying process.

Slip the leash on your dog and walk him around a bumper left lying on the kitchen floor. The moment he goes to grab it, yell "No! Leave it," and prevent him from reaching the dummy by snapping the lead. When he walks past and ignores the bumper, tell him "Good boy." Repeat this several times in a five-minute session. You can do this drill three times a day until your dog understands that he receives a "Good boy" for leaving it, and a firm "No" for making a grab. At the end of each session tell him to "Fetch it" and allow him to deliver the bumper to you. Eventually you will be able to walk him off lead around a bumper and have him ignore it until you say, "Fetch it." When he understands the meaning of "Leave it", you can move on to the next drill.

Sit your dog in front of you and flip a bumper backwards over your shoulder. As soon as he moves towards you, holler "No! Leave it," and place him back on the same spot. As you are standing between him and the bumper it should be impossible for him to make it to the dummy before you. The moment he settles down and stops trying to break whenever you throw the bumper, tell him "Good boy" to confirm that this is what you want.

After several sessions, your dog will begin to understand that unless he has been sent for the bumper, he is to remain seated, but don't become over-confident. If you allow him to beat you to the bumper, you will have reinforced his belief that everything on the ground is his by right.

Working with an assistant, you can eventually start throwing bumpers to the side or over your dog's head. Having someone to help will enable the bumpers to be collected quickly should your dog break. When this happens, give him a firm "No," and drag him back to his original spot and start again. Try always to finish on a positive note so that he feels confident rather than dejected.

Slowly, you can increase the level of distraction by moving to different locations and firing a blank pistol (away from your dog) whilst flinging bumpers or rolling tennis balls past him. If you have a training group, you can sit all the dogs in a circle and throw a dummy around, always watching for signs of breaking. If your dog is doing well, do not make a big fuss; this will only encourage him to get excited. Simply say "Good boy," and keep him settled.

Don't forget to give him a retrieve at the end of the session to let him see the difference between sending him for a dummy and breaking.

As soon as he makes this last retrieve, take the bumper from him and drop it in your game bag out of the way. Do not under any circumstances carry bumpers in your hands or pockets where they can be clearly seen. It's most unfair to have bumpers on open display and expect a young dog to walk quietly at heel.

Dogs are great readers of body language; therefore, it's

important when teaching steadiness that you walk slowly and speak quietly. Flinging your arms around like a maniac and yelling at the top of your voice is not conducive to the calm demeanor you are trying to encourage.

Training with other handlers and their dogs provides a great opportunity to teach steadiness. Make your dog honor quietly while shots are fired and others are sent to retrieve. Ensure that you are in a position to intervene if he attempts to break. I quite often use a second "leash" made out of fine twine that I loop around his collar and my belt. I take off his normal lead and let him believe he is unrestrained. If he tries to break, I'm on him like a ton of bricks, yelling "No," and shaking him by the scruff. When you employ such devious tactics your dog starts to show real respect.

In the entire steadying process, it's important not to overstep yourself. Alice was a twelve-month-old female Lab doing well in her steadying program until I grew cocky and threw half a dozen bumpers around her at the same time. She spotted her window of opportunity and beat me to a dummy; it took six weeks of hard work to steady her and repair the damage. Young dogs can really punish you for mistakes made in training

If you lack time, early morning can be useful for carrying out steadying drills. Have your dog on stay in the yard where you can see her through the bedroom window as you dress. Correct her with your voice whenever she shows any inclination to move but do be careful. (If the neighbors hear you shouting, "Keep still, girl, until I tell ya to move," through the bedroom window, it may unfairly damage your reputation.)

Once you have your dog rock steady on bumpers and gunfire, you can switch carefully onto birds. Expect to see your dog's excitement level move up a couple of notches and be prepared. No bumper in the world holds the temptation of a duck smacking down on the water or a plump pheasant flapping its wings as it falls from the sky.

You can start on cold game and change up to live birds as your dog learns self-control. All the steps you took steadying him on bumpers can be employed to do the same on the real thing. (A word of caution though: if you are going to fling dead ducks and pheasants around the kitchen, make sure the family are out for the day.)

One final word on steadying. Be sure that you always send your dog for a retrieve with the same command or he'll use your uncertainty as an excuse to break. That's

Once steady on bumpers and gunfire, you can switch to birds... but be ready to see a lot more excitement in your dog.

why I use "Fetch" when I want my dog to pick up something close by. I don't use his retrieve command for anything except casting him from my side.

When I send my dog, I call his name followed by "Get back." When you are working several dogs at the same time, using just a name is not enough. I want my dogs to listen for what follows. I may need to ask one dog to retrieve and another to sit down. I don't want the wrong dog to go just because he heard his name.

Be sure you say what you think you say. So often I hear the same handler shouting: "Get it boy," "Fetch it up," or "Okay," and then tell me that they always use the dog's name to send him. Little wonder their dogs break. If your commands are not crystal clear, you can be sure your dog will take advantage and act on his own initiative.

Learning to Swim
One morning last summer I was out at the kennels when I noticed my neighbor was hanging his brand new Armani suit from the washing line.

"How are you, Joe?" I enquired.

"Damn annoyed to tell you the truth, Vic."

"How come?"

"It's that bloody dog getting me in trouble again."

Joe has a large male Newfoundland, named Jake, who is as near to Homer Simpson as a dog can get.

"What's he done this time?"

Over the next hour, Joe gave me the long, sad tale of how he'd told his wife he was taking Jake for an evening walk while in actual fact, they were both nipping down to the pub for a few pints.

Jake and Joe are regulars in the Bulls Head and while Joe plays dominoes, Jake saunters from bar stool to bar stool looking for anyone soft enough to buy him a beer. Around midnight, they wandered back home along the narrow canal towpath with Jake weaving from side to side and Joe stumbling along behind, his wrist firmly entwined by the long slip chain looped around Jake's neck.

Unfortunately, Jake failed to negotiate a sharp bend in the towpath and stumbled into the black water, dragging the hapless Joe with him.

"So what did you do?" I enquired, genuinely eager to know what anyone did floundering in twelve feet of muddy water chained to a drowning dog.

"We couldn't get out at that point because the bank was too steep, so we decided to swim to the lock."

I was stunned. "Are you nuts? That must be a quarter mile swim."

Introducing your pup to water for the first time should be all about play.

Chapter Five: Formal Retrieving

"I'm telling you, Vic, it was frightening," Joe replied.

"I can well imagine."

"No, you don't understand. It wasn't the swim… it was the women!"

"Women, what women?" I was completely lost.

"A group of them, walking down the towpath in the pitch dark, smoking and chatting like it was the middle of the day. Only witches would do that? It was scary."

"Are you serious? I'll tell you what's scary, Joe. A drunk wearing an Armani suit, swimming down the canal in the dead of night, chained to a dog the size of a water buffalo. Now that is scary."

Fortunately, both Jake and Joe like swimming, but some dogs avoid it like the plague. There is nothing difficult about introducing a young dog to water. Choose a warm summer day and paddle in up to your ankles carrying a pocketful of treats. Give your pup a tidbit and throw one just in front of him in the water. As soon as he has it in his mouth, pitch another a yard ahead of him and continue until he has to swim to earn his reward.

Give him lots of encouragement and praise him for his efforts. If he is still reluctant to swim, you can call upon the services of an older dog to tempt him into the water. Blue is particularly skillful in this role and never interferes with nervous young pups once he has them in the water.

A narrow waterway or river is particularly useful for teaching a young dog to swim. If you can safely cross to the other side before having an assistant bring your pup to the opposite levee, you can encourage him across to you, but don't try this if your dog can easily find a way

Atom is on his way to becoming a great water dog.

around. Once he's learned he can avoid the water by finding an alternative route, he will constantly search for one.

It's not wise to do this in winter, as freezing water is nowhere near as inviting, so choose your time carefully. Never force your dog to swim or push him reluctantly into the water. You can create a bigger problem than you solve. Like his introduction to gunfire, teaching a pup to swim is an exercise in association. If he has a good time, he'll love it. If he has a bad experience he won't.

I really like having an older, more experienced dog available when I'm doing water work with pups. I can always count on an old hand to make it look like fun or use him to retrieve a bumper that's drifted away.

Personally, I'm not impressed with big water entries. I've seen too many injuries to regard it as an asset. As long as my dog will enter the water without hesitation, I'm happy. If he wants to feel his way in, it's okay by me.

Once you have your dog swimming freely, don't be

Chapter Five: Formal Retrieving

tempted to throw a bumper into the middle of the lake "to see what he'll do." What's going to happen if he won't bring it back? Waiving your arms and whistling until you are blue in the face will only convince him that water is the best place in the world to defy you.

Don't even attempt a water retrieve until your dog is making straight out-and-back retrieves on dry land. If he has still not grasped the concept on land, you can be sure he won't improve in water.

When he finally makes his first water retrieve, the temptation for him to shake and drop the dummy will be overwhelming, so before he does it, tell him to "Hold it" just as you did in Chapter Four.

Meet him at the water's edge and quietly take the bumper from him before he has chance to drop it.

Most retrievers really love the water, and will soon be diving right in.

You can teach him to shake on command, just as you taught him to relieve himself, by saying "Shake" precisely when you know he's going to do it and confirming it with "Good boy" the moment he complies.

When he understands that he must deliver before shaking, you can move farther back from the levee and insist that he delivers to hand. If he tries to drop the dummy, walk towards him and order him to "Hold it." If he drops it, say "No," replace it roughly in his mouth, and repeat "Hold it." He must be made very aware of his obligations.

Do not try to introduce your pup to water and teach a formal water retrieve at the same time. His initiation to water should be pure fun. The discipline of a trained water retrieve can come later, when he has more confidence.

Most dogs love water and once he's in you may find your pup reluctant to come out. Do not constantly blow the recall whistle while he swims around ignoring you. This is not a lesson you want him to learn. Try playing with a bumper yourself on the levee or, better still, bring out your older dog and do some retrieving drills close to the water's edge. Most young dogs will come back as soon as they think they are missing out on the fun.

If he refuses all attempts to entice him out of the water, simply walk away and hide. Sooner or later he's going to realize that he's all alone and panic. Don't rush to reassure him. Let him learn that it's not a good idea to let you out of his sight. Once he hits the levee, let him see you walking away, and as he approaches, slip his leash on in total silence.

Chapter Five: Formal Retrieving

I never allow my dogs to have a mass free-for-all in the water. Once they are out of control, anything can happen and this is often where new problems begin. If I want to let them cool off during a training session, I give each of them the opportunity to take a dip, but I never have more than one dog in the water at any one time. That way, I can supervise the whole activity.

Chapter Six
ADVANCED TRAINING

It's now time to find yourself a number of different training areas. Choose at least one with a straight fence along its perimeter.

Many of the drills you will do from hereon can be made so much simpler by having a straight fence or wall on hand. If you lack such a facility, look for a levee, pathway, or anything that will encourage your dog to run straight out and back. Also, you will need a deserted parking lot, so it's an early trip to Wal-Mart or anywhere you can find a safe expanse of black top. If you are questioned by security just tell them a mad Brit sent you — they'll understand.

Have you figured out where we are going? Okay, lets go.

The Stop Whistle
With your dog at your left side on his lead, walk in a straight line along the wall or fence (this will dissuade him from flaring out from your side). We have already taught him to sit when you stop, so halt, blow one long blast on your whistle, and raise your right hand. (Do try and buy yourself a British whistle — six dollars won't

break the bank, but it will save you from ear damage.) As soon as your dog sits, tell him he's a "Good boy." If he fails to sit, forget the whistle and go back to simply stopping and snapping the lead above his head until he sits every time you stop. (Review Chapter 4.)

Once he has thoroughly mastered the concept, walk on again and stop abruptly, blowing one long blast on the whistle whilst raising your right hand. As he sits down, say "Good boy" to confirm this is what you require. Repeat the drill for ten minutes, by which time he will start to associate a single blast on the whistle with sitting down. Next time, run along the fence doing exactly as before (think of all those calories you're burning), then halt suddenly as you blow the whistle. This will help speed up his response time. If you repeat this drill successfully for several days, your dog will be ready to progress.

Now do exactly as before but remove his lead. If he fails to sit on the stop whistle, you have moved on too quickly, so place him back on his lead and start over.

When you are convinced he understands, repeat the same process off lead as you did previously until he sits every time you halt. The next drill is to step in front of your dog, facing towards him, as you blow the stop whistle so that the picture he has is of you standing squarely in front of him with your right hand raised. Repeat this several times until he is familiar with the new picture.

Now you can begin to back away from him after he has stopped on the whistle to create distance between you. He needs to be made comfortable with stopping while you move away. You are about to take a significant

CHAPTER SIX: ADVANCED TRAINING

When your dog will stop and sit while you keep moving, then he's really understanding the stop whistle.

step forward, so don't rush. Make sure your dog really understands that one long blast on the whistle means "Sit" and that he's happy for you to back away.

On the next occasion you sound the stop whistle, keep walking; if you have read your dog correctly, he will sit on the spot as you stride away from him. Don't go too far — a couple of paces are sufficient. Now turn towards him and raise your right hand. If he moves forward, tell him "no," take him back to the exact spot where you blew the whistle, and blow it again in his face. Try once more and if he stops on the whistle, tell him "Good boy."

He's now starting to understand that the stop whistle means "Sit" whether you stop or not. This is an important concept he needs to assimilate before you can commence handling drills. If you can't stop him on command, he will be running around like a headless chicken.

Now walk at a brisk pace along the fence and blow the stop whistle without slowing down. Your dog should sit automatically as you stride away. Several paces on, swing around to face him with your right hand held high. If he has stopped successfully, you can do it on the run.

The next stage is to stop him as he comes towards you. Tell him to sit and stay, walk thirty yards away along the fence line, then blow the recall whistle. As he reaches the half-way stage, raise your right hand and blow the stop whistle. If he stops, go to him and tell him "Good boy." If he doesn't stop, drag him back to the exact spot where you blew the whistle, make him sit, and blow it again in his face.

Mix this up with some heelwork and retrieving or he will start to anticipate the stop whistle and come towards you at a snails pace.

Additional Stop Whistle Work
Now go grab some rocks about the size of tennis balls — we are going to learn him to stop in full flight.

Got 'em? Okay. Now with your dog walking beside you, toss a rock ten yards in front. Turn and walk back thirty yards along the fence away from the rock. Now send your dog, but before he's gone ten yards, blow the stop whistle. If he stops, all is well and good. If he doesn't, get after him and haul him back to the spot where he should have. There is no bumper out there so he's not going to be rewarded with a retrieve if he refuses to stop. Once you can stop him in full flight, you will know that he really does understand the stop whistle and you can be a lot tougher if he gives you a refusal.

Again, mix this drill up with others or he will become reluctant to leave your side, always anticipating the stop whistle. Practice stopping him when he is hunting or when you are working on handling drills.

With practice, you should eventually be able to stop him anywhere at any time, but don't go from kindergarten to college overnight. As the distance between you and your dog increases, so does the temptation for him to ignore you. Move to longer distances slowly.

Just because you can stop him at twenty yards does not mean he will stop at two hundred. Every time he ignores you, get on his tail and drag him back. You don't want to have to do this too often so that's another good reason for

When trained correctly, a retriever will calmly sit and stay until you command him to move.

doing things gradually. If you manage his progress correctly, you will rarely have to run out two hundred yards to chase him down.

Remember, if he is in long grass, near running water, or upwind of you, he may not be able to hear your whistle, but don't make this an excuse.

Only blow your stop whistle once or your dog will learn to obey on the fifth or sixth attempt when he thinks you might enforce it. Any time he willfully ignores you, get out there and make him comply.

Finally, here's a great tip I learned form an old timer. In training, only blow your stop whistle at half volume, keeping something in reserve for when he's in the field and temptation overwhelms him.

Hunting the Area

As a young man, I was offered my first opportunity to pick up on a prestigious country estate with my brain-dead flat-coat, Rex. The estate was run for the Lord of the Manor by a doughty Scottish gamekeeper renowned for his disciplined approach and fiery temper.

He instructed me to stand behind two gunners, neither of whom had dogs of their own, on the edge of a stubble field. My job was to collect anything they shot.

Some gamekeepers want birds collected as they fall while others prefer them to be left until all the shooting is finished.

"Do you want me to pick up during the drive or wait until it's over?" I enquired.

"Do as you please, laddie, but dinna let your dog go into that field of sugar beet. His Lordship wants to shoot

Chapter Six: Advanced Training

Guns and beaters on a shooting day.

that this afternoon and he'll expect to see plenty of birds. I dinna want them disturbed until I'm good and ready."

With this warning ringing in my ears, I led Rex to a spot sixty yards behind the gunners. I had decided to hold him back until the drive was over and pick up afterwards, but the guns had different ideas. No sooner had they begun shooting than they called, "Picker-up. Get a dog on that bird."

Considering his wayward tendencies, Rex performed his duty admirably until one of the guns failed to shoot an easy cock pheasant. In order to cover his embarrassment at missing such a simple shot, he shouted, "That bird's a runner, send your dog."

There was no alternative. I had to comply, but Rex wasn't convinced. He sloped off in the direction I pointed without enthusiasm. Fortunately, I had seen a cock, shot earlier, fall into a peat bog nearby. I intended to hunt Rex in the area and let him return triumphant with the alternative bird. I knew the gunner in front would be happy if we helped maintain his reputation.

As Rex approached the small bog, he shook his head in disgust at the foul smell emanating from the peat. "Hi-Loss," I called, instructing him to hunt up. Rex waded tentatively into the peat.

The bog ran adjacent to a small wood and rather than hang around in the oozing mud, Rex decided to explore further afield.

After five or six tense minutes, I blew my recall whistle but with no result. The gunners in front were dropping birds everywhere and calling for a dog, but Rex had gone absent without leave.

Thankfully, everyone was occupied when I saw him in the distance darting across the forbidden sugar beet in hot pursuit of a pheasant. I closed my eyes and prayed to God that he returned before anyone spotted him.

The gamekeeper's whistle finally blew to confirm the end of the drive and my gunners were sheathing their shotguns and comparing notes when Rex appeared, proudly holding his bird aloft.

"Damn fine show, " shouted the errant marksman, accepting the bird I handed from Rex's mouth. "Shot it up the backside, must have flown on a bit. Bloody good dog you've got there, old chap."

During the afternoon, the beaters were called upon to walk the sugar beet while the gunners waited in eager anticipation for the birds to be driven over them. Not surprisingly, there were few birds to be found. Rex had

Chapter Six: Advanced Training

cleared the area of everything worth shooting. I was just grateful that I was the only one who knew. It was our secret.

At dusk, as we gathered to count the day's bag, his Lordship appeared complaining furiously that the drive across the sugar beet had been "very disappointing." He fixed me with an accusing stare and I felt my mouth go dry.

"Any idea why there were no birds?" he asked.

"I think a fox m-m-might have disturbed them," I stammered.

"A fox in broad daylight? I doubt that very much, young man."

"Aye, he's right," intervened the gamekeeper, "I spotted a fox in there ma self just before lunch."

"Yes, well in that case, I'm sure that's the reason. Just make sure it doesn't happen again. Damn disappointing." His Lordship turned abruptly on his heels and left.

I was still trembling when the gamekeeper came over and handed me a brace of pheasants in payment for my day's work.

"Do you have any wildlife books at home, Sonny?" he enquired.

"Err... yes, one or two," I replied.

"Well, see if you can find any reference to black foxes roaming the English countryside."

"Black foxes?" I repeated, somewhat puzzled. "How big?"

"Oh, let me see now... About the same size as your dog."

He winked and I blushed with embarrassment before jumping into my old truck and beating a hasty retreat.

After that, I swore to teach my dogs to hold the hunt area. Any retriever that gives up after a few seconds and runs off wherever the notion takes him is an embarrassment.

"Hunt Dead" (How to Train)

You should have decided on your hunt command ("Dead Bird," "Hunt Dead," etc.) and taught your pup its meaning in the yard searching for tidbits. It's fun with a young pup to hide treats and tell him "Dead Bird" until he finds one. That will give him a basic understanding, but now we need to progress him to the next level.

Without your dog knowing, hide a bumper in cover, walk him right up to the area, and tell him "Dead bird" (or "Hi-Loss" if you want to speak like a Brit). Encourage him downwind of the bumper so that he scents it, but do not allow him to wander too far from the area. You don't want him galloping all over the field only to stumble upon the bumper by accident on his way back. That's not the lesson we are trying to teach him.

The moment he grabs the dummy, praise him lavishly with an enthusiastic "Good boy." After a few repetitions, he will learn that "Dead bird" means there is something to find. If you have an understanding wife (or husband), next time you mow the grass in the yard leave a ten-foot circle uncut. That way you have a well-defined hunt area in which to hide your bumpers.

As your dog becomes more confident, you can hold him in the area longer by asking him to hunt for a tennis ball. This takes considerably more effort and you should spit on it (my Southern friends will love this) before you hide it to give him a reasonable chance to detect some

Chapter Six: Advanced Training

scent. None of the objects you hide should be visible; we are trying to teach your dog to use his nose.

Once he has been taught to hunt around your feet, the next stage is to teach him to hunt at a distance.

Find a small patch of cover, walk him to it, and sit him down. As you cover his eyes with one hand, toss a bumper into the cover. Command him to "Wait" and back up a few paces. Blow the stop whistle, raising your right hand (you

Even birds stuck up trees need to be retrieved.

will see why later). Now give him the "Dead bird" command. The chances are he will move towards you, so arrange things so that the scent from the bumper is blowing towards him tempting him to hunt. Help him as much as he needs, but again, do not let him leave the area until he finds the dummy. The whole idea is to show him that wherever you give the "Dead bird" command is the best place to hunt. Praise him as soon as he picks up the bumper and let him deliver it to you. After some practice, he will realize that he can find things on command without being at your side. You can now do the same exercise with a tennis ball (don't forget to spit).

The final piece of the jigsaw is to teach your dog to run to the hunt area from your side and search where you tell him. This is how to do it.

Let him see you drop the bumper in the patch of cover and walk him away thirty yards. Now send him back. As he reaches the cover, raise your right hand and blow the stop whistle. When he has been sitting for ten seconds, call "Dead bird" and let him find the dummy. As soon as he can do this with ease, swap the bumper for his tennis ball.

Now, this is where it gets interesting. Grab yourself a small rock and this time drop the rock in place of the ball,

It takes a great deal of experience to retrieve a hare.

Chapter Six: Advanced Training

but send him back, stop him, and tell him "Dead bird." He will start hunting for the ball but he won't find it, and he will be convinced that you are wrong. He will want to leave the area, but do not allow him to do this. Stop him and make him hold the area, but when his back is turned, throw the tennis ball into the cover.

Watch his surprise as he finds a ball in the precise location where he has already searched. He's now starting to think that maybe you are worth listening to.

When your dog can be handled left, right, backwards, and forwards, you can refine this drill by sending him 100 yards for a non-existent tennis ball. Every time he moves out of the area, you can handle him back onto it and hold him there. He will be convinced that there is nothing to find, but have a helper standing close to the cover ready to drop a ball on your signal. Your dog will want to give up and move off to hunt farther afield. Give your assistant the signal to drop the ball, then handle him back to the area. Once he returns, stop him on the whistle and give the hunt command. Contrary to what your dog believes, this time he will find the ball. Now he is convinced that you are a genius.

The Hunt Back Whistle

Often, your dog will overrun the fall area, so it will be necessary to teach him to hunt back towards you. We do not want him to confuse this with recall, so take him back to the fence. Sit him down quietly, tell him to "Wait," and back away from him along the fence line. After ten yards, drop a bumper in clear view but keep walking a farther ten yards.

With the bumper between you and your dog and in stark contrast to the rapid blasts of the recall whistle, blow several slow peeps and encourage him to come towards you and collect the bumper. As soon as he picks it up, tell him "Good boy." The fence is important to ensure that the bumper is directly in his path, but a wall or any straight walkway will do.

This drill will teach him to hunt towards you, but we want him to do so with his nose fully engaged. (Unlike recall when we expect him to forget his nose and simply race back as fast as he can.)

Once he is competent collecting the bumper, switch it for a tennis ball, but don't hide it. Leave it on the path in open view. Remember, it's a very small object with little scent, so he will have to approach cautiously or he will pass right over it. When he picks up the tennis ball, praise him and encourage him to come to you.

As he progresses, you can make finding the ball increasingly difficult by placing it in longer grass, but don't forget we are trying to teach your dog to hunt towards you, so don't start hiding it thirty yards to his left or he'll miss it.

As he gains confidence you should be able to sit him anywhere in the field and have him hunt towards you on the "hunt back whistle." I tend to keep the peeps going until he reaches the ball.

As his confidence grows, you can sit him down, throw a bumper directly behind him, and hide a tennis ball in front. Then you can either send him back for the bumper he has seen or command him to hunt towards you for the hidden ball. His comprehension of this drill will tell you just how much he understands.

CHAPTER SIX: ADVANCED TRAINING

I never stop teaching my dogs how to hunt. Even Blue gets to do these drills on a regular basis, although he has been known to switch the agenda and come back with a rabbit.

Handling Drills

For many of the earlier drills, a straight wall and a parking lot were desirable, but for early handling drills, they are absolutely essential. We want to make these early stages as easy as possible and the absence of grass will help enormously. Make sure you use your cleanest, whitest bumpers.

With your dog sitting two or three yards in front of you with his back to the wall, throw a bumper along the wall to your left.

Here I'm teaching Daz the "Get out" command.

Now, raise your left arm straight up above your head and blow the stop whistle. Then stretch out your left arm like a traffic cop and call "Get out." (You could call "over" like a true American, but you may run out of commands if later you want to teach your dog to jump over fences.)

If your dog sits like a statue, move up close to him and try again. Make sure you have his attention, then move your arm slowly in the direction you want him to go. The moment he moves towards the bumper say, "Good boy." Don't try to stop him breaking until you are convinced that he will go every time. Once his enthusiasm has been established, you can make him "Wait" until you give him the command.

If he now hurtles out for the bumper each time you tell him, start throwing it to your right. Sit him down, blow the stop whistle, raise your right hand straight above your head, then stretch it out to your right and call "Get out."

I can hear you asking, "Why blow the stop whistle if my dog's already sat down?" Oh ye of little faith.

It's to teach your dog that when he's at work, a stop whistle will always precede these instructions. Think about it — you'll have to stop him to handle him. Satisfied? Good, let's move on.

So now he will go left on command and right on command... you think... And regardless of what I say, you are going to throw two bumpers, one to the left and another to the right, and guess what? Your dog is now totally confused. Okay, let's help him out. We are going to reintroduce our old inanimate friend, the rock. If your dog does go the wrong way, he's not going to get a reward.

Chapter Six: Advanced Training

Throw the rock to the left, then toss a bumper to the right, making sure you throw the bumper last. Now blow your stop whistle, raise your right hand vertically above you, stretch it out slowly to the right and call "Get out." If he goes in the wrong direction, shout "No" and call him back to his original sitting position. Pick up the bumper on the right, but this time toss it closer and make it as tempting as a squirrel dumpling to a Mississippi farmer.

Now try again. If he even glances in the right direction, call "Good boy," and when he picks the bumper give him lots of praise.

Now reverse the process, throwing the rock to the right and the bumper to the left. When he is consistently making the correct choice, you can dispose of the rock and use two bumpers, but be warned. If he takes the wrong cast and beats you to the bumper, your training will go backwards. Retrievers may be smart, but it takes thousands of repetitions to perfect left and right casting.

Once he's really proficient at lefts and rights, you can introduce a straight back. This time, leave your dog sat sideways against the wall, but instead of you moving away from the wall, walk along it but away from your dog. After ten yards, turn to face your dog (see Diagram 3).

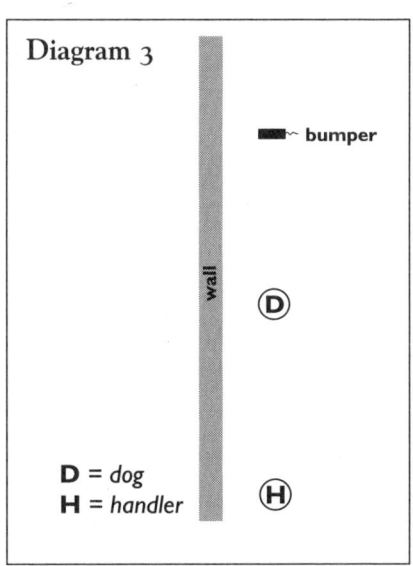

Using a straight wall to teach your dog to "Go back."

145

"Get back"

Toss a bumper over his head, then raise your right arm vertically and blow your stop whistle. Keeping your arm upright, wave it backwards and call "Get back." If your dog bolts back and picks up the bumper, all is well and good. If he doesn't, you will need to tempt him and reward him with praise for making the right decision.

When he is dashing back on command every time, reintroduce a right-hand bumper so that now you are asking him either to "Get back" or "Get out" to your right.

Make sure you send him for the last bumper first and make it as tempting as possible. This is the way to guide him into making the correct choice. It all helps to communicate what you want.

Finally, you can use three bumpers. Ideally you should have a couple of assistants to pick up a bumper quickly in case your dog makes the wrong choice, but failing that use one bumper and two rocks.

Now that your dog has the idea you can change locations, but don't start throwing your bumpers into cover.

Chapter Six: Advanced Training

Your dog is still learning and when he turns to look in the right direction, it will help if he can see the bumper.

Incorporate handling drills in his daily training and once you are sure he thoroughly understands your hand signals, make sure he complies.

In my Wednesday gundog classes, I often tell handlers to pair up, asking one of them to be the dog and the other the handler. The handlers are then told to cast their "dogs" to a distant mark known only to the handler. The results are often hilarious. One poor guy got unwittingly "handled" off a steep levee into a lake, while another ended up underneath a truck in the parking lot. If your training buddy can't follow your hand signals, what chance does your dog have? So before you give your

Casting left

Casting right

retriever a hard time for taking an incorrect cast, make sure that your handling technique is not to blame.

When you are convinced that your dog thoroughly understands casting, you can place two dummies in clear view (one left and one right) and cast him back for a blind, but plant a number of blind bumpers behind him so that when he takes the cast, he cannot help but find one. Now do the same with the blind planted to the right and the seen bumpers behind and to his left. When your dog will take the cast to a blind every time, you know that he really understands the concept, but it is very important that you plant enough blind bumpers to ensure he always finds one right away. It will speed up his understanding and save him from confusion.

Teaching Blinds

Macclesfield, the place where I live, is probably one of the wackiest towns in England. Recently, we had a thief who tried to escape from a police high-speed pursuit vehicle by diving into the river with a jacket full of stolen antiques. He didn't get very far.

Following a domestic altercation, a local man appeared in court claiming that his wife had attacked him first by grabbing his genitals. He then attempted to prove it by showing his bruised testicles to the entire court.

Not long ago we had a bunch of thieves who stole a set of midwives' uniforms. God knows what they intended to do with them? For months, residents lived in fear of being at the bank when a gang of midwives burst in screaming, "This is a cesarean. Lie on your back with your legs in the air and no one will get hurt."

CHAPTER SIX: ADVANCED TRAINING

Each year is a vintage one for bizarre events and I always start the New Year thinking that the previous one will never be surpassed, and I'm always wrong.

Each summer a local charity holds a Bike-a-thon in which cyclists ride a tough course along a prescribed route for sponsorship money. The event always draws a big crowd and starts from City Hall where the police chief makes a speach on road safety.

This year, the police went one better and provided a Road Safety Trailer, inviting cyclists inside to watch safety videos and collect accident prevention leaflets before the start of the event.

Macclesfield City Hall stands at the pinnacle of one of the steepest inclines in the county, but unfortunately the police forgot to place chocks under the wheels of their trailer. No sooner had the cyclists left the town center than the huge cravan broke away from its moorings and overtook them as it hurtled downhill, flattening everything in its path. Finally it came to rest in the wrecked premises of... wait for it... the oldest cycle shop in the county. Thankfully no one was seriously injured but can you imagine the fun residents will have retelling this story to future generations?

So what's all that got to do with teaching blinds? Very little. I just thought you might need a break.

Making a Start
If a stranger suddenly appeared beside you and pointed North and shouted your name, would you go? Neither will your dog. But suppose you had an inkling that after a couple of miles you might find a bag of cash, what then? You'd be off like a shot.

That is the principle of running blinds. Your dog has to believe that wherever you point, he will find something of interest to him.

So with your dog at your side, start by dropping a bumper at the end of a straight fence line. Turn and walk away as you have done before. When you are fifty yards away, send him back. Do this half a dozen times each day, dropping the dummy in exactly the same spot every time. (Lets call it the "Drop Zone.")

When he's hurtling back without hesitation, leave him in the truck and this time, go drop the bumper in the

Teaching a young dog to run a blind (note the fence).

CHAPTER SIX: ADVANCED TRAINING

Drop Zone. Nothing has changed except on this occasion your dog hasn't seen you do it. Take him to the fence, point him towards the bumper just as you did previously, and send him. If you have set it up correctly, he will rush back to his usual place and collect the bumper.

If the picture has changed in any way — there's a drainage ditch recently been dug across his path or a tree has fallen in his path — he may have trouble, so start again.

The idea is to present him with a familiar picture and a routine that he already knows leads to a reward (the bumper).

Once he is running back on command to collect his dummy, you can start moving away from the fence line and pointing to the Drop Zone from different locations, but let him see you drop the bumper the first couple of times before you try running him "blind."

Now find a number of alternative Drop Zones in different locations and repeat the process from stage one, allowing him to see you drop the bumper and establish the routine before you run it as a blind. These locations will become recognized in your dog's mind as permanent blinds, i.e. places where he knows he will always find a bumper.

When your dog is confidently racing out for all his permanent blinds, you can start cold blinds. These are random blinds where your dog has no previous knowledge. You are simply pointing him in a particular direction and asking him to go. The success of your early attempts will depend upon:

- His drive and self-confidence.
- His belief in you.
- How you set up the blind.

I find the easiest way to begin cold blinds is on a straight footpath where I can scatter a number of bumpers before I get my dog out of the truck.

After I collect him, I walk him along the footpath to within twenty yards of the unseen bumpers. I point down the path and send him back. Although the bumpers must not be hard to locate, I don't want them clearly visible either. He must not be able to see them when I line him up or it isn't a blind. Sometimes, if the path is bare, I cover the bumpers with a handful of grass.

Pointing him into a light breeze with the scent from the bumpers drifting towards him is a great help, so check the direction of the wind. Do not try and send him into a Force Ten headwind. (He isn't training for Air/ Sea Rescue).

You want your dog to have instant success to help him understand the concept. The moment he heads off in the direction you indicate, he should run straight into one of the bumpers. That's why I wouldn't recommend you start this in an open field where there is too much opportunity for him to run in the wrong direction and become confused.

Try and find locations and conditions that make going back and finding his bumper easy. There's a wonderful canal (inland waterway) where I live with a towpath once used by shire horses in the 1800s to pull boats laden with coal and American cotton. This is a great place for teaching blinds.

I park close by, work out the wind direction, then place my bumpers in various locations along the towpath. I go back for my dog and point him down the towpath, knowing that he will run straight into one of the bumpers.

As soon as he discovers the dummy, I praise him and whistle him back. We walk along the towpath for a while, then I stop, point ahead again, and send him. Less than twenty yards into his stride he finds another bumper. By now he's beginning to think I'm David Copperfield; every time he goes where I point, he finds a bumper.

Remember, you are trying to build his confidence; distance at this stage is unimportant. After several weeks of success on these short blinds, he will go at will in any direction you point. You can drop a bumper unseen behind you in an open field, then send him back from twenty yards, but check the wind direction to ensure it's in his favor. As you start to increase the distance, go back to the path or fence where he can understand that success comes from running in a straight line. We will talk more about this when we discuss Straight Lines later in the next chapter.

So let's just review where you should be. If you have managed to restrain yourself and not jump from step one to step ten, your dog should now run short (twenty to thirty yards) cold blinds or a long permanent blind without difficulty.

You should be aware of the importance of the wind on blinds, always trying to use it to your dog's scenting advantage. Later we will discuss the effect of the wind on other aspects of your dog's work, but for now if you remember to always work him downwind of the bird/bumper, you will make his learning so much easier. Don't forget to pepper the Drop Zone with bumpers so that he can easily find his reward. In this drill, we are not teaching him to hunt; we are asking him to go on command in any direction we point. The more bumpers you leave, the more chance he has of success.

Learning to Mark

I know you have been waiting for this so let's get right to it.

The reason for leaving it so late in your dog's development to work on marking is to prevent the breaking and noisy anticipation you hear in the duck blind or cornfield almost every hunt. Believe me, it really isn't necessary for a brilliant marker to have hundreds of marked retrieves. You have already taught your dog to sit quietly and resist temptation; it's now time to let him learn how to mark.

By far the best method is in a "walk up." For this, you will need at least three other training buddies with their dogs and a field of grass short enough not to completely hide the bumpers.

Space yourselves about twenty yards apart with your dogs at your sides, making a straight line stretching sixty yards across. Arrange for everyone to carry a blank pistol and a bag of bumpers. Lets call our handlers Tom, Dick, Harry and you. Agree to the order in which each handler will fire.

On your command of "Walk on," have the entire line move forward at a slow pace. Without warning, have Tom fire a shot and throw a bumper twenty yards in front of him. All the dogs should be made to sit to shot.

Now, Harry can send his dog for the bumper thrown by Tom while the remaining dogs honor. Once Harry's dog

Chapter Six: Advanced Training

The start of a "walk up."

has made its delivery, call "Walk on," and after the line has travelled a further twenty yards, fire your pistol and fling a bumper in front of you as all the dogs sit to shot. This time Dick sends his dog for the retrieve.

Continue in this manner until all dogs have had four retrieves, which will be more than enough. Each dog will have seen sixteen marks, but as they have only been sent for four, they will have had experience of honoring another dog's work. Always be prepared for your dog to break. Do not hold him back on his leash or he won't learn a thing. Have a second lightweight lead made from twine and keep interchanging it with his regular lead until he doesn't know whether he is on leash or not. Wait until he sees the bumper hit the ground, then remove his normal leash — if he's going to break this is when he'll do it.

Let him go rocketing out and then… Wham! You will have him on the end of the twine and you can shake him by the scruff and growl "No" at him until he decides it wasn't such a good idea. A word of warning: be sure to loop one end of the twine through his collar and the other around your waist or you risk the twine cutting into his neck or slicing through your hand.

This is an opportunity for you to establish the rules, so do not tolerate squeaking or whining.

The great thing about a "walk up" is that you can teach your dog to mark while reinforcing his heelwork and showing him how to behave in company.

As your dogs understand what is expected, you can extend the marks by stretching the line out so that each

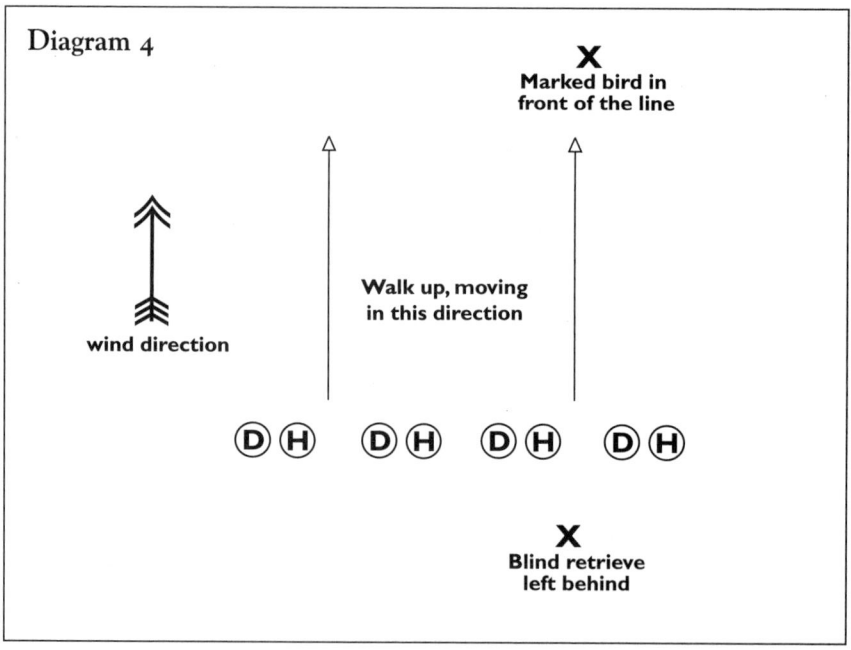

Let your dog see the mark, then send him for the blind.

Chapter Six: Advanced Training

dog has a longer retrieve. Later you can each use a dummy launcher instead of throwing bumpers to send the dogs much farther out.

Once your dog is totally steady, you can start asking for the occasional "blind." This is how it works:

As the line walks along, Tom leaves an unseen dummy behind near a suitable landmark (tree or weed). The line carries on, marking and retrieving bumpers. Your dog then sees his mark thrown in front, but this time you tell him, "Leave it" and turn him around, pointing him towards the blind behind. Make sure the bumper is not too far away and send him from downwind to give him a good chance of finding it. While you are working your dog, all the remaining dogs have to honor and resist the temptation to go for the bumper thrown in front (see Diagram 4).

When your dog returns with the blind, Dick gets to send his dog for the dummy previously thrown in front. This will test both his dog's memory and Dick's ability to mark the fall.

With practice, you can stretch your line across a river or a gully, with half the dogs on one side and half on the other (see Diagram 5). You could position yourselves on opposite sides of a small lake or have six or eight dogs in the line if you wish. There is no end to the variety of retrieves you can manufacture in a walk up and, because each dog has to wait his turn, he is learning to mark and honor at the same time.

If you are an upland hunter, it will be a great advantage to have a steady dog that will sit to shot. Duck hunters can organize their walk up so that every retrieve is in or across water. Imagine how useful it will be to have a

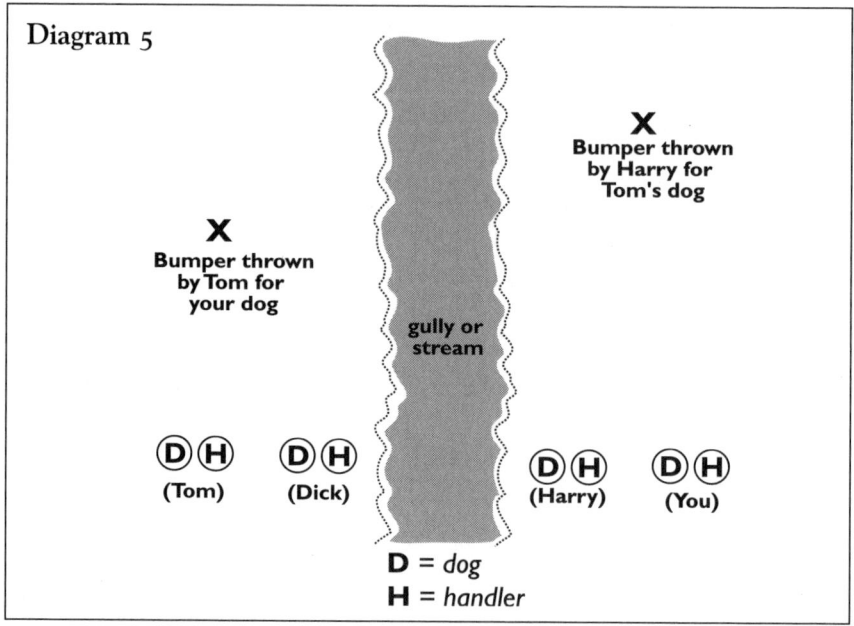

Having a walk-up line at either side of a river or gully gives dogs the opportunity to negotiate obstacles.

dog that is used to marking, honoring, and making multiple water entries.

Using a walk up for marking practice does not prevent you from giving your dog more specific marking drills later, but it is an excellent way to introduce marked retrieves without risking his steadiness.

Live Birds & Cripples

There is no mystery about introducing your dog to game. If he is already retrieving bumpers to hand and understands the "Hold" command, the rest is easy. A few live pigeons is all you need to get him started.

Do everything exactly the same as you did when giving him a mark, but replace the bumper with a shot

Chapter Six: Advanced Training

pigeon. If possible shoot it as a flyer so that it will be fresh. This is not a marking drill so make it a real easy retrieve into light cover (not in the open where he can see it flapping around).

Let him hunt it up in his own time. Don't interfere unless he leaves the area altogether. This is his first bird and he will want time to investigate and gain confidence. As soon as he picks, it give him lots of praise and encourage him towards you. If he doesn't pick it, don't panic. Collect it yourself and let him sniff it in your hand. Shake it around to stimulate his interest, then toss it back into the light cover. If he dashes after it, let him go. Don't

There's no mystery to introducing dogs to birds — they love them!

make him wait to be sent. If he breaks, we can sort that out later when he knows what's required.

I have gone through the process of tying wings to bumpers and using artificial scent, but to be frank, I found it a waste of time. I have never had a retriever that didn't like real birds better than anything on earth.

Once he's confident with shot birds, you can show him how to track cripples by sending him for a wing-clipped pigeon in cover. Very few dogs have the confidence to pick these the first time, so be patient and let him work it out for himself. Don't start hollering and whistle-blowing; it will just distract him. Give him quiet encouragement when he looks to you for guidance.

We have already taught him the hunt command, so use it to confirm what you want. When he does eventually pick the bird, encourage him towards you and don't be in a hurry to take it from him. Prevent him from parading around you by backing up to a wall, fence, or anything that stops him from walking around in circles holding onto his "prize."

As he comes towards you with the bird, command him to "Sit." He knows what that means and you can insist on compliance. Stroke him on his chest and under the chin to encourage him to lift the bird up to you instead of hanging his head.

When he is proficient on pigeons you can use the same method to introduce him to other kinds of game, always allowing him time to investigate the new scent.

You can expect your dog's enthusiasm to move up considerably on live game, so it's important not to let him have every bird that falls from the sky or his steadiness

CHAPTER SIX: ADVANCED TRAINING

Eight-year old Field Trial Champion Angus at the end of a long day.

will evaporate. If you can organize a walk up shooting live pigeons thrown into the air instead of bumpers, so much the better, as he will have to wait his turn and honor the other dogs. Once again, do not tolerate whining.

It is very important to organize these training sessions with care. The last thing you want is another dog breaking and ripping the bird from your dog's mouth. That will not encourage him to hold his birds gently.

Once you have your dog working reliably on live game, you need to ensure that his earlier training doesn't go out the window. So here's what to do. Your dog will always want to go for the last bird down, but don't allow him to have it. Turn him away and insist that he goes for a blind in a totally different location. Don't make it too difficult. Plant a few birds in the area of the blind so that he finds one easily. Eventually, he will realize that following your instructions leads him to the Promised Land.

The worst thing you can do is give your dog a lot of easy marks where he can see the bird flapping about in the open. Pick these yourself or I guarantee he will start breaking.

Wing-clipped pheasants are very good for teaching young dogs to track cripples, but they run fast so don't delay too long before sending your dog or the bird will be out of state. Try not to interfere with his hunt unless he goes hopelessly wrong, in which case, handle him back onto the scent.

Let him track the bird and if he fails to pick it, don't despair; he's just learning his trade. Send an older, more experienced dog to collect it. Next time you are on a hunt and another dog brings back a cripple, turn it loose and let your dog track it. He has to know what to do.

My young dog, Stan, is a phenomenal marker but in his first season, he just could not work out what to do when he made it to the fall and the bird wasn't there. He had to be given the opportunity to learn with my old dog Blue providing back up for any cripple that got away.

A lot of people ask if teaching dogs to hunt unshot and wing-clipped game encourages them to chaise birds, and of course it does — until they learn from the ones

Chapter Six: Advanced Training

that fly away which birds are worth pursuing and which aren't.

If you have done all your basic groundwork correctly, introducing your dog to game is no big deal — just switch bumpers for birds and let him work it out. I find that a lot of very keen young retrievers are halfway back with a shot bird before they realize it's not a bumper.

Last night I took Daz, my fifteen-month-old yellow Lab, for a walk up in sugar beet. He'd never seen a partridge in his life, but he retrieved a couple of shot birds with very little fuss. He did fail to pick a cripple, but after tracking it for five minutes, one of my training buddies slipped a dead bird in behind him and he picked it with ease.

After that, I had him walking to heel and sitting to shot as the other eight dogs did the work. He came home just as steady as he went out, but with his confidence to pick partridge boosted considerably.

Next time out, I'll give him another try on a cripple and see if he has the confidence to pick it. Once he's had a few more dead birds and gotten used to hunting in the sugar beet, I doubt he'll have any problem.

Chapter Seven
DEALING WITH OBSTACLES

Lining & Cheating
I think it was George W. Bush who said in his 2001 election campaign, "You can fool some of the people all of the time and these are the ones I'm gonna concentrate on."

Well, there's no point in me trying to fool you. If lining your dog like a laser beam is really important to you, a Brit is not your best advisor. There are dogs trained in America that can be aimed with the accuracy of a S.A.M missile; however, to show you what can be achieved without the aid of an e-collar, I thought I should cover the topic.

Your dog will always be inclined to run in the direction he is facing, so before you even think about lining, you must have a dog that will come squarely to heel whatever way you stand. If you already have a good heeling dog then teaching him to pivot with you in any direction is easy.

Simply sit him at heel with his leash on and turn 180 degrees; call "Heel," and the lead will help you guide him into position. Now keep turning until you are back at your original position and say, "Heel." When he adjusts himself correctly, let him know by telling him "Good boy."

After a few repetitions, instead of turning 180 degrees, move in quarter circles (90 degrees), each time telling him to "Heel." Start off moving clockwise and when he has mastered this move, counterclockwise. Repeat this drill regularly and you will soon have a dog that sits squarely at heel whatever direction you face.

The next step is to teach your dog that he must go wherever you send him, so start by pitching a couple of bumpers into the open thirty yards away in completely opposite directions. Send him for the second one last. After a few days, he will work out that he must go for the bumper you indicate. You can then reduce the angle between the bumpers by throwing them at 90 degrees to each other.

He will now be tempted to switch bumpers on the outrun but don't allow it. Shout, "No!", clap your hands and recall him to indicate this is not what you want. Do not stop him on the whistle or he will start running back to you every time you blow the stop whistle. Shorten the distance if necessary so that you have more control. When you can confidently send him for whatever bumper you indicate you can add a third dummy (see Diagram 6).

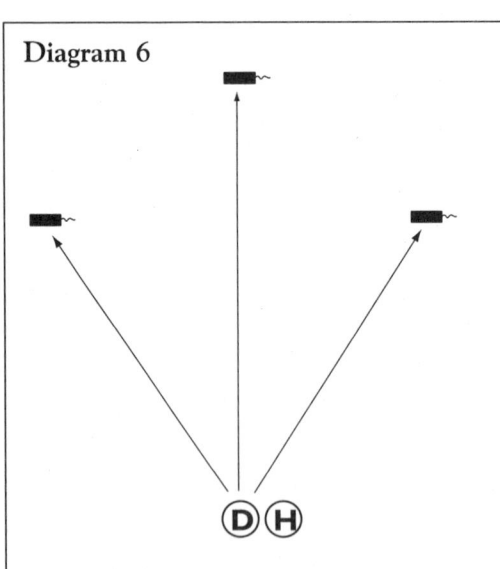

Diagram 6

Add a third bumper and move close enough for your dog to understand which bumper you want.

Chapter Seven: Dealing with Obstacles

Once again, make it simple. Go back to the Wal-Mart parking lot if you wish, where the dummies will be clearly visible. Do anything that helps him to follow your instructions. Do not at this stage toss your bumpers into heavy cover and turn three simple marks into a multiple blind. To quote my old school teacher, "It's not big and it's not clever."

You are trying to build your dog's confidence by teaching him to go where you point and receive a reward (a bumper). Use the biggest bumpers you can find and the shortest grass.

Okay, your dog will now take a straight line to three different bumpers. You can now begin extending the distance, but slowly, slowly. The best lining drill I've seen was shown to me by Mike Stewart at Wildrose Kennels. He uses a "ladder" of bumpers to extend the lining distance. Start with the first bumper twenty yards away, then five more bumpers at ten yard intervals in a dead straight line. Each time your dog makes the retrieve, send him back on exactly the same line until he collects all six bumpers. You will be amazed how quickly he will learn to run longer, straighter distances.

At some stage you will need to send him over obstacles, which he would much rather go around. This is where the British and American trainers part company. In Britain, a serious trial dog is allowed to use his judgment. He's not permitted to bank run or avoid jumping a fence, but he can make his approach from the most advantageous angle. But, alas, not in American Hunt Tests or Field Trials. In these events, he's expected to run in a dead straight line.

By shortening the distance again and making it simple, you can teach your dog to do this. Typically, I run this drill with the help of a training buddy and a small fence in the yard. I pitch a bumper on the far side of the fence, then send my dog from a very short distance away. If he attempts to go around the fence, I holler "No" and my buddy picks up the dummy. Then I call him back and start over. If he goes straight over the fence, he gets the bumper. He learns that a direct approach gains him a reward and an attempt to run around gets him zip.

You need to set this up so that the temptation to cheat (run around) is built up slowly. I usually start with a very small fence and a dead rabbit instead of a bumper. Labs love rabbits and the scent they give off is sufficiently strong to almost drag them over the fence. (Provided you have taught your retriever to jump beforehand.) I discuss more difficult jumping later in the chapter, but it is very important when teaching a young dog to jump that you wait until he is at least twelve-months old. You can ruin the hips of a growing dog easily by aggressive jumping.

If your dog really has a problem knowing how to jump, simply walk him over the fence a couple of times. If necessary, sit him a yard from the fence, stride over to the other side yourself and call him to you.

Once he has the general idea, you can send him from a few yards away for the rabbit or bumper. Then progress a little farther back so that eventually he will take a straight line over the fence from thirty yards away for a bumper placed just over the far side of the fence. You can then reverse the process by sending him from close to the fence for a bumper ten, twenty and eventually thirty yards on the other side.

CHAPTER SEVEN: DEALING WITH OBSTACLES

With patience, you should be able to send him from thirty yards away and have him take a straight line to a bumper thirty yards on the far side. Once he has grasped the concept of a straight out-and-back approach, you need to keep the temptation to cheat minimal and the desire for the retrieve as high as possible. Use birds rather than bumpers to increase desire and build up to the more difficult retrieves step by step. You will need a couple of helpers to prevent your dog cheating and still getting his reward.

A great tip I learned from my good friend Jim Dobbs is to use white channel flags at each side of the obstacle as gates to show your dog that he must pass between them and not run around them. Once he learns this in the yard he will have a better idea of what is expected when you have them placed out in the training field. Also, make sure your help is in place at either side of the gate to prevent him cheating (see photo).

Setting up white "channel" flags on either side of an obstacle will help your dog understand that he must go directly over the fence.

169

If you get careless or over-confident with your set up and your young dog learns to cheat and still get a reward, it will take a lot of convincing to straighten him out.

Take a look at the diagrams. I hate complicated theory, but I think we need an illustration here for clarification.

Dealing with Obstacles

I always find dogs a lot easier to train than their handlers. Last week my new summer class began and I talked my wife into throwing a little party on the first evening for the participants.

"Do you like scampi?" she enquired of one of my pupils.

"Oh yes, I love all those Walt Disney films."

I knew I was in for a difficult summer.

Your retriever is not a piece of machinery. He's a living, thinking character with his own take on the world in which he lives.

He understands that running downhill is easier than uphill. He knows that plowing straight into the wind takes more effort than dealing with a cross wind.

Ditches, cover, fences, and ice-cold water all make demands on a working retriever, and if he enjoys early success by avoiding them, he will remember. What thinking dog would want to jump a high fence or negotiate a deep gully if he has previously found it to be unnecessary?

Inclines

The natural reaction of your dog to inclines is to bend with the slope. If you ask him to make a retrieve across a hillside, he may shoot off in the direction you indicate but

Chapter Seven: Dealing with Obstacles

as he moves farther away, his course will drift downwards with the slope. In Britain, the handler simply makes allowance for this natural "bending" in the line he indicates. He uses his handling experience to determine which initial direction will result in his dog arriving at the bird (See Diagram 7).

If you aspire to Hunt Test success, this is not acceptable and you will need to break out the white flags and place your "gates" in a direct line to the bird.

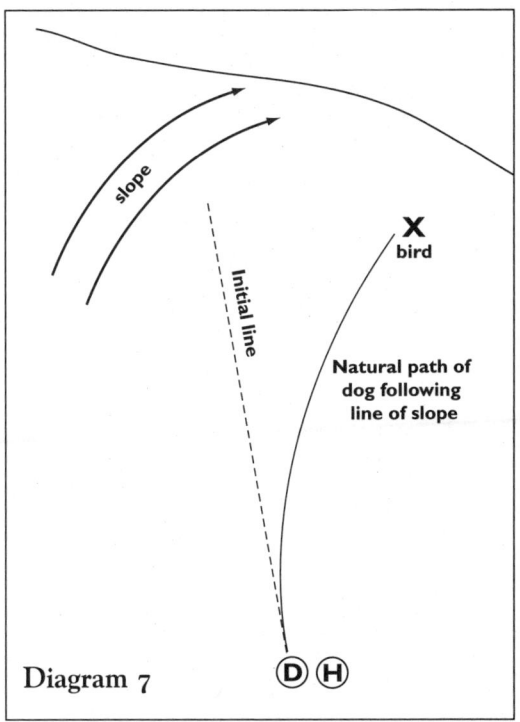

Cast your dog to make allowance for the contour of the ground.

Wind

Retrievers do not like to run directly into the wind and will naturally slow down much quicker running into a headwind; something you need to take into account when teaching blinds.

You can teach your dog to run into the wind by laying down a ladder of bumpers, requiring him to go directly into a headwind. Once again, make haste slowly and do not place the bumpers in cover. This is not a hunting drill — we are simply trying to teach your dog that he can obtain a reward (the bumper) by running directly into the wind. We want him to be comfortable and confident when he feels the wind in his face. Slowly extend the distance you are asking him to cover and make it easy for him to succeed.

Crosswinds evoke a completely different reaction and you will find that your dog "bends" with the wind exactly as he did when negotiating slopes. This time he will "bend" downwind in the same way he "bent" down the slope. Experienced retrievers learn to use this to their advantage, knowing that moving downwind of the line you ask them to take will give them a better chance of scenting the bird.

Once again, British handlers make allowances for this tendency when sending their dog and ask him to take a line significantly upwind of the fall, knowing their dog will drift on the wind and hit the fall area (see Diagram 8). Hunt Test guys just have to get out those white flags and lay a line of gates to train their dogs to run straight through them even in a cross wind.

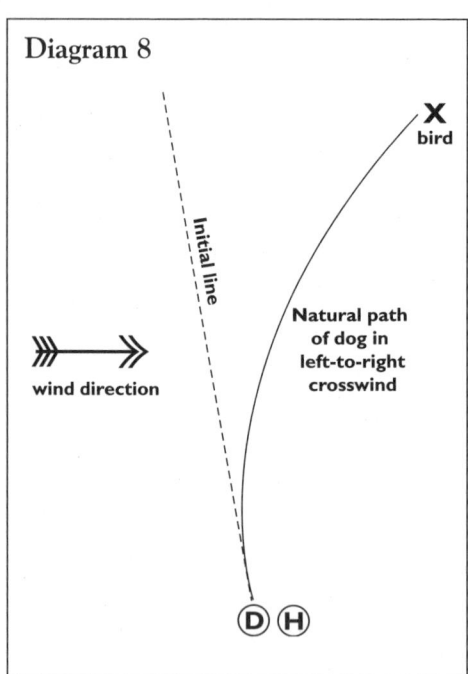

Cast your dog to make allowance for the wind.

Old Scent

The scent of game from a previous fall is guaranteed to attract the attention of a young retriever, and handling him off it can present a problem.

Once your dog is confident running out on marks and blinds with enthusiasm, you should start training on distractions. Before you let him out of the truck, take a shot bird and rub it into the grass at the halfway stage of a cold blind (one he has not run before). Cover a large enough area to ensure that he cannot fail to run over it. The scent left behind will be considerable. Now take several birds and drop them twenty yards beyond (see Diagram 9). If possible, organize things so that he will be running into the breeze.

Now go get him and run the blind. I guarantee he will stop to investigate the scent you created. Blow your stop whistle and when he sits, cast him back. The moment he turns in the right direction, shout "Good boy." If the scent from the blind is drifting towards him, it will help him understand that

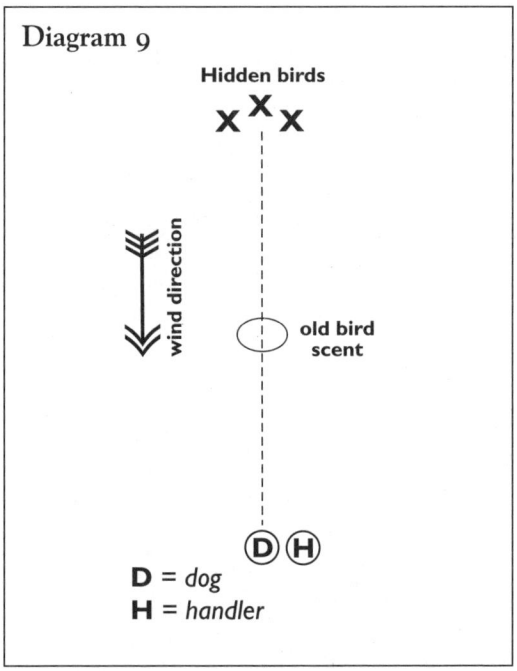

Young dogs are always reluctant to leave bird scent, even when there is nothing to be found. Run this drill to convince him otherwise.

there is bird behind him and make moving him off the old scent a lot easier. If he is really reluctant to leave the old scent, it might be worth giving him a minute to prove to himself that there is nothing to find.

If he struggles to comprehend, make the drill a lot easier by stopping him on the old scent, then have a bird boy attract his attention and drop a bird behind him. He will race back to collect it. Once he has the idea, remove the bird boy and change back to a blind.

Ditches and Gullies

The natural inclination of a young retriever is to hunt the valley of a ditch rather than cross it. If he has early success finding birds in this location, it will further convince him there is no need to climb the other side.

Some early marks on the far side of such obstacles will give him the incentive to go straight across. As he descends the gully he will lose the mark, and when he appears on the far side, we want him to find the mark easily, so make sure you have plenty of bumpers planted in the location so that he cannot fail.

Once he realizes that his reward lies on the opposite side of the gully, he will gladly make the journey. Now you can set it up as a memory and let him see you drop a bumper, then walk him to the opposite side. When you send him, he will undoubtedly go hurtling back across the gully for the dummy. After several repetitions, you can set it up as a blind. Check which way the wind is carrying the scent and plant your bumpers accordingly. You want him to climb that bank and scent a bumper with ease, so plant several dummies so that he runs right into one of them.

CHAPTER SEVEN: DEALING WITH OBSTACLES

When he has experienced repeated success in different locations, you should have no problems sending him across ditches and gullies.

Jumping
Fences and walls provide natural boundaries which dogs learn to observe. Unfortunately, game birds don't share the same respect for ground-based obstacles and continually fall inconveniently on the far side.

Remember, it is important that you wait until your dog is

This young dog is looking for help behind a high fence.

at least twelve-months old before teaching him to jump. You can ruin the hips of a growing dog easily by aggressive jumping.

Just as we don't want our young dog to have a bad early experience in water, we must avoid any unpleasant accidents when teaching him to jump. A dog that finds itself frighteningly entangled in a wire fence on his first jump will not be eager to repeat the experience.

Stone walls such as this are common in England.

The easiest way to tempt your dog to jump is by you climbing over a small fence and encouraging him to follow you. Most young dogs will happily negotiate a two-foot fence to be with their owner. Once he can do this, flip a bumper over for him to retrieve.

Next move to a higher fence and repeat the process. It doesn't take long for dogs to gain confidence, but as the obstacles become more formidable, you need the help of a training buddy.

If you toss a bumper over a high wire fence, there is a possibility that your dog will get himself caught up, particularly when he is returning with a large object in his mouth obscuring his judgment.

So use a tennis ball and have your buddy standing by the fence ready to assist if your dog becomes entangled. Under no circumstances must you risk having him dangling with his back legs trapped in the wire. That is how hips become dislocated.

Once he is hopping over confidently with a tennis ball, change to a puppy dummy, moving up slowly to a full-size bumper, a Droken Duck, and finally a dead bird. Remember that when he comes back holding a bird, he may have a wing covering his eyes, so stand by to help out. Use praise and encouragement — pressure does not work in these circumstances.

In British trials all dogs are expected to jump, and frequently have to negotiate a six-foot stone wall while carrying a hare, but if you build up your dog's confidence step by step you will have little difficulty.

Hedgerows and Dense Cover
Britain has thousands of miles of hedgerows so learning how to deal with them is an absolute necessity. North America may not have the same preponderance of natural boundaries, but the method for negotiating them applies to any patch of dense cover.

The principle is very similar to the one used in teaching your dog to jump, but on this occasion your dog must be encouraged to push through the cover in the same place, both out and back. Running around looking for an opening is not acceptable.

Start where the cover is not too difficult to penetrate and let your dog see you push a bumper to the far side. Preferably, you should pass the bumper through the same gap that you expect your dog to take. If he only has to pass one yard through the cover to retrieve his bumper, it will suffice to teach him the principle.

Send him through the gap and as soon as he picks the bumper, encourage him back to you the same way. If he tries to find a new gap, discourage him with a gruff, "No." After a few repetitions, mark the gap with the white flags on each side as previously described and send him from ten yards out with the bumper in the same place, just a yard on the far side. Do not permit him to go outside the marker flags.

As soon as he can go out and back through the same opening, you can extend the distance by standing farther back from the cover. Each time encourage him to come back to you exactly the same way he went out.

Summary

All these drills for negotiating obstacles must be re-taught in numerous different locations before your dog truly

Blue at full throttle.

CHAPTER SEVEN: DEALING WITH OBSTACLES

understands what is required. Each time you change location, go back to the beginning. If he becomes confused, do not continue. Take him back to a point that he understands and start over.

Whether you are training for competition or for hunting, it is important to teach your dog how you want him to deal with obstacles. You may require a straight line or be prepared to tolerate him "bending" with the terrain or wind, but do not allow him to simply run around searching for the easiest route. Not only can you lose a lot of birds, quite often there just isn't a less challenging option and you will have a dog that doesn't have the confidence to go for the retrieve.

Make your training progressive and learn to read your dog. Don't let him lose confidence — help him out or go backwards and repeat lessons he knows if needs be. Plan your training sessions carefully before you take him out of the truck so that you don't rush into it only to find that your set-up is flawed and the entire lesson wasted. Pay particular attention to the direction of the wind; unlike other obstacles, it varies from moment to moment and can fundamentally change your dog's performance.

Being aware of your dog's likely reaction to each obstacle is more than half the battle. Work with him to show him what's required and your teamwork will improve tenfold.

Chapter Eight
WATER WORK

Before you try to run any drill on water your dog must be 100 percent on land. There is absolutely no point expecting him to be competent at anything on water if he is less than perfect on dry land. Remember, it's going to be a lot more difficult to correct him once he's in the lake. Assuming that he has been thoroughly schooled on land, you can now start from scratch in the water.

Water Entries
Before we get down to the nitty-gritty, can we dispel the great American myth of big water entries? It may look exciting on television, but it is not very smart. I have never seen an experienced British Field Trial Champion that threw itself headlong into a stretch of unknown water.

Some young dogs just have to do it until experience teaches them otherwise. My old dog Blue is an exceptional water dog. He's been brought up on the shores of a lake. I've watched him buck waves for 300 yards to collect a mallard, but he's far too experienced to dive head first into the unknown. Blue may love rushing into the water, but

The big water entry is not necessary in a retriever; your dog simply needs to be willing to enter water without hesitation.

he does so with his brain engaged. If you have ever seen a dog speared on an underwater pole, or heard one scream as it dives onto a barely-submerged barbed wire fence, then you understand the danger.

If your dog naturally has big water entry, then you'll just have to let him learn. If not, then be thankful. All your retriever needs is a willingness to enter water without hesitation. You don't have to encourage your dog to launch himself into outer space.

Here endeth the first lesson.

Simple Retrieves
As with every training session, think your water session through before allowing your dog out of the truck. Ask yourself how easy will it be for your dog to run around the

Chapter Eight: Water Work

water instead of swimming straight out and back? A small circular pond is no good for what you are about to do. Its far too easy for him to cheat.

Think of any obstacles that might interfere with your dog's concentration? An aggressive gaggle of geese swimming nearby could give him a really bad experience.

Start with a straightforward single, but don't allow him to go hurtling into the water as soon as he sees the splash — we want to teach a water retrieve, not develop a breaking habit. Make sure you have a few rocks in your bag. (What's the betting that after this book is published gundog stores around the U.S. will start selling rocks via mail order?)

Now with your dog sitting quietly by your side, fire a blank shot and toss a rock into the water. Don't stand for any whining or barking. After your dog has settled, repeat the process. If he is overly excited, don't give him a retrieve at all; just fire a few shots, throw your rocks, and let him get bored waiting — then put him back in the truck.

Try again a few days later until he can sit and wait without too much fuss. Once he has learned to be patient, then fire a blank and toss a bumper. Count to ten, then send him. As soon as picks the bumper, blow the recall whistle and encourage him back towards you.

He will find it a great temptation to drop the bumper as he comes out of the water, but you are not going to let that happen, no sir. You, my friend, are about to wade into the water to meet him and take the dummy gently from his mouth as he approaches.

When he leaves the water, he will undoubtedly want to shake and as he does so, say "Shake" followed by,

"Good boy" just as you did earlier. This will confirm that this is what you want.

After a few sessions, your dog will begin to understand that his job is to make his delivery without dropping the dummy, and then shake. You can now move back to the levee and insist that he delivers to hand. If he attempts to drop the bumper, call "Hold it." He has no excuse; he has already been taught the meaning of "Hold." Continually dropping the bird on water retrieves is one of the hardest habits to break in a mature retriever. Don't allow it to develop.

Remember, if he attempts to shake before delivery, call "No" and make him deliver to hand. Once you have the bird, watch him carefully and call, "Shake" exactly as he shakes, followed by, "Good boy."

Teaching a dog to "Shake" on command is easy; just say "Shake" when the dog is about to shake anyway, and soon he'll understand what you want.

Chapter Eight: Water Work

Handling Drills

Once you have a *perfect* single retrieve, you can commence work on handling drills. For this you need some shallow water, a good pair of waders, and a retractable lead.

Stand in the water and pitch a bumper fifteen yards out, then send your dog who is attached to the extendable lead. When he is half way there, blow your stop whistle. If you have done your job on land he should turn towards you, and as he does so blow the recall whistle and call him back.

Now send him again, but this time don't stop him — allow him to make the retrieve. Keep mixing up the drill and repeat it up and down the levee, with him never knowing whether he is going to be stopped or not. This will teach him what the stop whistle means in water. If he becomes reluctant to go, it is simply an indication that you are stopping him too often and he is anticipating the stop whistle. The remedy is simple; just let him have a few sessions where you don't stop him at all.

Remember, you have him on an extending lead, so you have every chance to enforce your stop command. If he refuses to acknowledge it, get after him, growl and shake him. If he continues to ignore the stop whistle, go back on dry land and practice.

Once he shows genuine understanding you can pitch a couple of bumpers twenty yards apart. Send him for the last one you threw first, then stop him half way and cast him towards the other one. If he's casting well on land he should have no difficulty, but if the water causes initial loss of confidence, make it easier by sending him for a rock and casting him towards a bumper. (Useful things, rocks.)

Soon he should be stopping and casting in the shallow water for these short retrieves. Do not now start sending him halfway across Lake Michigan. This is a sure way to sabotage his water handling. Build up the distance slowly so that you can use your voice to control him if he does go astray, exactly as you did on land.

Just in case he is tempted to swap birds on water, you may want to repeat the drill we used on land in the shallows where you can maintain control. Flip him a couple of birds initially twenty yards apart. Send him, and call him to you as soon as he picks the first bird. If he shows any interest in the second one, shout "No! Leave it."

Gradually reduce the distance between the birds until he will swim straight out, grab one bird, and ignore the other. Once again, do not put him in a situation where he can cheat repeatedly and get away with it. You may have to use the extended lead to maintain compliance, but if he's already been through this drill on land, I doubt it.

Introducing Decoys

When you have him handling confidently on water you can introduce him to decoys. It really is very simple. Set up the decoys in the yard and run a few easy retrieving drills. Send your dog through the decoys to pick up a cold bird. Most retrievers find this exercise a no-brainer and will ignore the decoys completely after a couple of runs.

Now repeat the same drill on water with a cold bird. Decoys do not carry anywhere near as much interesting scent as a duck and it won't take many repetitions before your dog swims straight to the bird.

CHAPTER EIGHT: WATER WORK

Most dogs will ignore decoys because they don't hold much interest when compared to a bird or dummy.

To be honest, all the hard work needed to handle your dog on water is done on land, and if you have worked diligently and followed the simple steps I've outlined, you should find the transition to water relatively easy.

Lining Drills
When you have him handling really well on water, you can begin your lining drills. For this, your choice of location is absolutely vital. Take a good look at the layout and ask yourself where your dog will be inclined to cheat. Small stretches of water are useless for early lining drills

Your set up is the most important part of this exercise. If you get it right, your dog will instinctively do it correctly. If your set up is flawed, he will not be able to resist cheating.

Initially, you want an uncomplicated out-and-back

retrieve at right angles across a stretch of water. I always start by having a training buddy throw me a mark on the far shore so that my dog becomes accustomed to going straight across instead of swimming around in the water looking for a bird. Once he gets the idea, I make it a permanent blind and start moving down the levee so that my dog has to swim at an angle back to the bird.

Step by step, I make the angle more acute and as I have already programmed my dog to go directly to the bird and straight back to me, his temptation to cheat is considerably reduced (see Diagram 10). Any time he looks like cheating, I blow the stop whistle and cast him away from the shoreline.

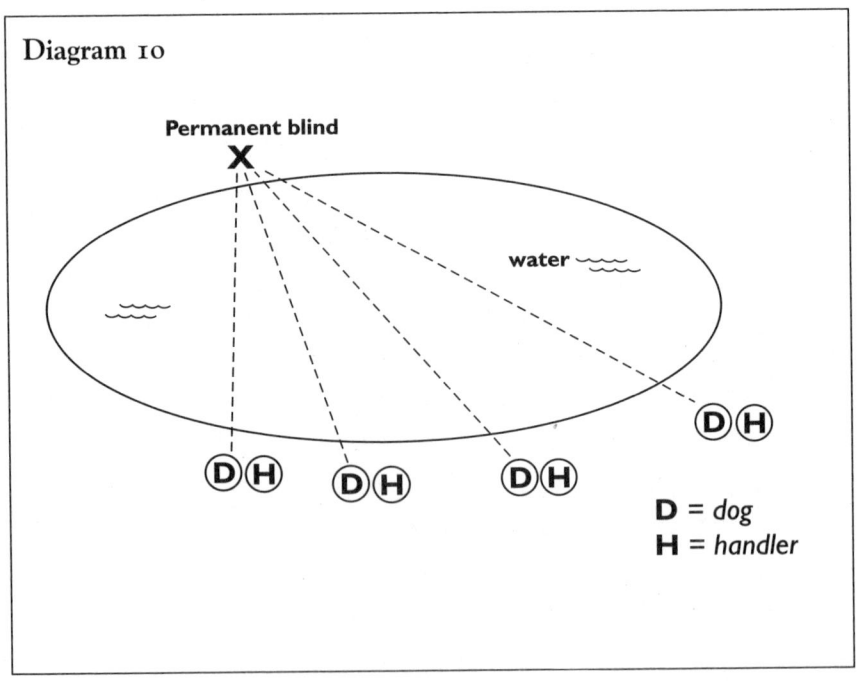

Lining on water — step by step, make the angle more acute.

Chapter Eight: Water Work

To build confidence, it's important in water work that your dog does not fail at what you ask him to do.

It is impossible to teach this successfully unless your dog will handle. You can't give a dog instruction from the far side of a lake if he won't stop and take a cast.

In British retriever trials, the dog is expected to enter the water without hesitation and take a straight line to the bird, but he may come back by the fastest route. If you are not running hunt tests, you may want to consider this philosophy. Imagine how quickly your dog loses body heat swimming out to retrieve those ducks in the depths of winter. If he can make it back to you quicker by hitting the bank and running the shore line, why not? You get the job done quicker and he has less chance of hypothermia.

Teaching blinds across water is precisely the same as on land. Set up your permanent blind from a short distance, then extend it step by step. If you have taught your dog to run through the white channel flags, you can use these to show him the route he must take to the water (see Diagram 11).

I usually start my first water blind from the same spot my dog had his marked retrieves. He has already experienced success in that location and needs little encouragement to return, even if he hasn't seen a bird thrown. Once he realizes that by simply going where I point enables him to find a bird, he is well on his way to running water blinds.

It is very important in building his early confidence that your dog doesn't fail, so set up your drill to ensure

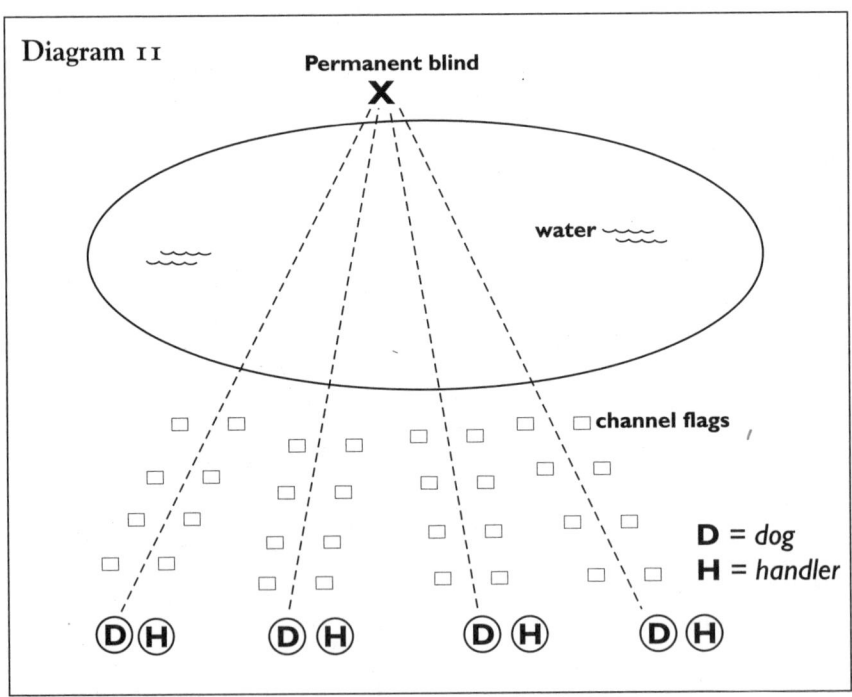

Using white channel flags to show your dog the line he must take.

Chapter Eight: Water Work

success. Often a young dog is reluctant to swim all the way across to the far shore, so I ask my training buddy to throw a mark and be ready to help out.

If he sees my dog is not going to reach his side of the lake, my buddy attracts his attention and entices my dog onto the mark. If that doesn't work, he throws another bumper. If that proves fruitless, my buddy pitches a dummy into the water in full view of the dog

Ben makes his water entry between the white markers.

and as close to the shoreline as possible. The splash usually pulls the dog onto the dummy and draws him almost to the far shore. It doesn't take long for a confident dog to learn to swim all the way across.

Once your dog has the out-and-back principle thoroughly engrained, the corner of a small stretch of water is very useful for teaching lining drills. You can pitch a bumper across the corner and ask him to swim there and back using your firm voice to apply pressure if he is tempted to cheat.

Finally, I use stones to teach my dogs to ignore distractions as they return with a retrieve. I begin by tossing rocks into the water and firing a shot as they swim back, and holler, "No" if they try to investigate. After a while they learn to ignore the rocks and the shot.

I then exchange the rocks for bumpers, maintaining the same routine, and finally I throw cold birds until they just ignore everything around them and deliver their bird.

If you are throwing a bird as a distraction, you must use another bird for the retrieve. Asking your dog to retrieve a dummy and ignore a falling duck is like refusing a date with Julia Roberts to go out with Hilary Clinton.

Duck Blinds and Boats
Young dogs need to be tutored in the art of working from boats and duck blinds, but it's not rocket science. All they

Expect a lot more excitement from your dog once you switch from dummies to real birds.

need is some good early experiences. You can encourage a young pup onto a boat with a few treats. Let him play around and hunt for tidbits among the paddles and decoys.

Now push the boat gently out into the water, hop in yourself, and let it drift. Hide a few treats around the boat so that he will want to explore every nook and cranny. When he appears happy and relaxed, take him for a little boat ride but make it fun. Do not try to force him into anything. Let him enjoy.

Similarly, with duck blinds, all you have to do is make him comfortable with entering and leaving the blind. Introduce him to the duck blind after he has learned to swim. With a young pup that has no fear of water, it's easy. Just use tidbits to encourage him into and out of the blind. Make it a game so that he is happy to enter and leave without any anxiety.

Soon boats and blinds will become familiar territory and working from them will be second nature.

Chapter Nine
QUARTERING & FLUSHING

I have a confession to make: Everything I know about training retrievers to quarter and flush I learned in America. Let me tell you how it happened.

I was delivering a valuable consignment of British Labs to my good friend Mike Stewart over at Wildrose Kennels in Oxford, Mississippi, when an enormous Tennessee trucker asked me, "How many British Labs will quarter and flush?"

"Err. . . quarter and flush. . . Let me see now…" I hesitated.

"C'mon, man, how many?"

"How many stars in the sky, how many fish in the sea?"

"Quit stalling, man, how many?"

"Taking into account the percentage loss and percentage gain and factoring in the differences in terrain I'd say. . . "

"How many?"

"None."

"None?"

"Well it's not something we do with Labradors in England."

"How do y'all find them birds in the fog?"

I was tempted to point out that fog had ceased to be a feature of the British climate since Edison invented electricity, but smart-mouthing a wild-eyed, 280-pound trucker didn't sound like a bright thing to do.

"We use spaniels," I replied lamely.

"Well get yerself over to Arkansas. There's an upland Hunt Test on this weekend and go see how it's done."

No less a person than Tupelo Deputy Police Chief Bill Gibson agreed to drive me there himself, whether to protect me from rednecks or deliver me on a plate he didn't say, but by five o'clock Sunday morning, we were on the road.

"Traveling light, ain't ya, boy?" he enquired, inspecting my clothing.

"It's too warm to wear anything but shorts," I replied innocently.

"Y'all know anything about chiggers over there in England?"

"No, can't say we do."

"Didn't think so," and he settled back in the driver's seat with a smile as wide as the Mississippi River.

After laughing themselves senseless at my lily-white legs, the members of Pin Oak Hunting Retriever Club were extremely helpful and allowed me to walk with the judges as their Hunt Test progressed. It was clear to see that upland hunters have to teach their dogs extra skills. I returned to England determined that the next batch of retrievers I sent over should be able to quarter and flush.

Ten days after I arrived home I began to feel unwell. I was uncharacteristically listless and what's more, I had an exceedingly sore butt.

Chapter Nine: Quartering & Flushing

"Why are you fidgeting around on that chair?" my wife asked as I ate dinner.

"I think it might be a good idea if you took a look at my backside," I replied uncomfortably.

"Before I eat dessert or after?"

By the time she left the table I was already laying face down, naked on the bed feeling sorry for myself.

"You are not going to ask me to jump off the wardrobe dressed as a nun are you?" she giggled.

"Stop fooling around and tell me if I have a boil on my butt will you?"

There followed a number of "Mmms" and "oohs" accompanied by some painful prodding and poking.

"Just a minute. I'll get the magnifying glass," she explained, dashing to the bathroom.

I was daydreaming when I felt an excruciating pain of such severity I was sure I'd been shot with a dart.

"Got it! Will you take a look at this?"

"What the hell have you done to me?" I yelled.

On this occassion, I at least dressed accordingly and wore long pants.

197

"Oh, don't be a baby. Look."

She passed me the magnifying glass revealing a giant Arkansas tick writhing in the claws of her tweezers.

"Do you realize that for the past ten days that thing has been gorging on your blood and living up your…"

Mercifully, I passed out before she finished the sentence.

Originally I thought the price I had paid for my initiation into upland retriever work was enough, but I was wrong.

At every workshop I run there is always a bunch of good ole boys who can't resist telling everyone about the Brit who got "ticked off" in Arkansas, or a couple of smirking duck hunters asking to see my "Arkansas hunting shorts." I don't know where they get

Upland hunting with a retriever can be very rewarding for both you and the dog.

CHAPTER NINE: QUARTERING & FLUSHING

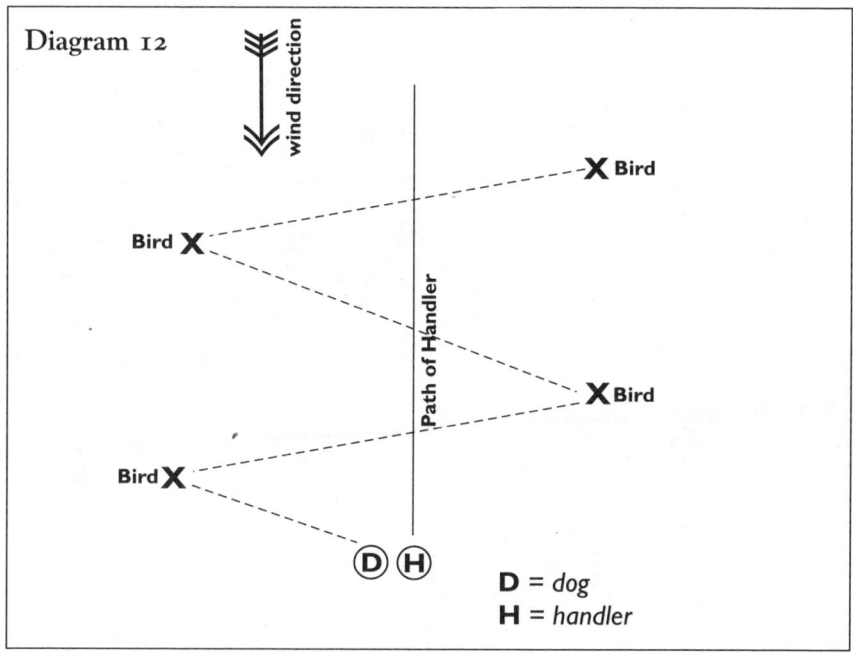

Encourage your dog to hunt from left to right and from right to left.

their information, but Tupelo's Deputy Police Chief swears it isn't him. (He also swears that he knows the whereabouts of Elvis.)

The role of the retriever in upland hunts is to point, flush and retrieve, and I've found it to be relatively easy to train young dogs to perform these functions.

You must first have a dog that has been through sound basic training and will stop on the whistle, cast left and right, and understands the hunt command.

Initially, I lay out two lines of birds or bumpers in front of me in light cover, the first line thirty yards on my left and the second line thirty yards to my right (see Diagram 12). I usually leave a space of about twenty-five yards between each bird.

A cold day of upland hunting for this golden.

I then walk down the center of the two lines and give my dog the hunt command, encouraging him to quest in front of me. I know precisely where the bumpers are and by pointing my left hand towards the first bird, I encourage him to find it.

Once he has delivered the left-hand bird, I cast him off to the right, giving the hunt command again. If he goes too far right, I give a short single peep on the whistle and point to his left, and to his total surprise he finds another bumper. Every time I need to turn him left or right, I peep my whistle and point. At this stage, it is very important that he is successful so check the direction of the wind. A following wind will encourage him to quest too far in front.

Always aim to work into the wind where he will be naturally inclined to hunt from side to side. If he drifts too far in front, I blow the recall until he's back in range. By using my voice and whistle, I try to ensure that he finds the nearest birds first and doesn't go charging out ahead to collect a distant bird. This is a quartering lesson and allowing him to forge too far ahead would be counter-productive.

I then send him off again to the left in the same manner and after a few days of such repetitions, he learns that by listening for the peep and following my hand signals, he always finds a bird. When he is really proficient at this, I slowly reduce the number of birds, making him work harder.

Introducing Birds
Next I introduce my dog to the bird launcher and walk him towards it, commanding him to sit as I release a live pigeon. This works better if the dog is working downwind so he has no warning of the bird being released and has to sit on sight.

Once he understands that he must sit on flush, I return to the previous drill, but replace the cold birds with live pigeons in multiple bird launchers and hunt them up in exactly the same manner. Only this time as the dog approaches, I release the bird and order the dog to sit. At this stage I introduce gunfire, but I only shoot blanks so there is no temptation for my dog to break.

When I have run this drill in several locations and know that he is rock solid, I will shoot the occasional bird without giving him a retrieve. I want to be absolutely sure

I can rely on him to sit on flush and remain steady regardless of the fall. Finally, I allow my dog the occasional retrieve but never without a pause. I don't want him to start to anticipate and undermine all his training.

When you make the transition to the hunting field, it's wise not to allow your dog too many simple retrieves — far better to pick these yourself. Even the steadiest dog will start to break given repetitive retrieves. Why ruin a good dog by sending him for birds you can easily pick up yourself. Save him for the difficult ones you can't collect.

Effects on Lining

As I've trained more retrievers for upland work, I have noticed the effect on their lining. Dogs that previously went out straight as an arrow on 200-yard retrieves sud-

Daz adds another cripple to the bag.

Chapter Nine: Quartering & Flushing

denly become ragged after a lot of quartering. Therefore, don't take it out on your dog if he does likewise.

I'm not saying that you can't work your dog on upland and water, but his lining will not be quite so impressive if he has to keep switching.

Just out of interest, I taught my old dog Blue how to quarter. Man, he thinks it's the best idea ever to cross the Atlantic. He can't believe that he actually gets to roam around unfettered hunting up pheasants. For most of his life he's had to watch spaniels and bird dogs do this right in front of his nose. Blue loves the American way, but he hasn't hunted his way across Arkansas wearing shorts, has he?

Chapter Ten
YOUR FIRST SEASON

I just heard our Prime Minister say in an interview that he was going to apply some "Blue Sky Thinking" to Britain's soaring crime figures. In view of his brilliant decision to ban all handguns, resulting in a forty percent increase in armed robberies, I assume "Blue Sky Thinking" means thinking unclouded by logic.

We don't want "Blue Sky Thinking" to undermine everything you and your dog have worked to achieve, do we? So when your first hunting season together finally arrives, what will be your strategy?

"Strategy. . . is this guy nuts?" I can hear you.

After all that effort, I know you just want to get out there and hunt; it's only natural, but it's not smart. Not unless you want to see all your training go down the pan. Let me explain.

Every drill you have run so far has been artificial. You have tried to simulate hunting conditions as close as possible but the real thing is still going to blow your dog's mind. All working retrievers move up several gears when confronted with the "real deal." No matter how well trained, the adrenalin coursing through their veins makes them impervious to the whistle the first time they see birds falling from the sky. Some well-schooled youngsters look like they've never had a day's training in their lives. Therefore, you're going to have to decide what's more important to you, duck or dog?

It's impossible to fully concentrate on your retriever and shoot at the same time, unless you tie him up, which will teach him absolutely nothing. It won't show him what you require or how you expect him to behave — it will just prevent him from breaking.

My suggestion is to let your buddies do the shooting while you school your dog (keep reading; it gets better). Stay quiet and calm, which will encourage your dog to do likewise, and be prepared for him to break. Use a second lightweight leash as we discussed previously to trick him into thinking he is unrestrained; then if he breaks, you can correct him. He may whine, so jump on it immediately.

If you are working upland game, it's even more important that your dog has your full attention — you want to stop him quickly if he gives chase. Don't overwhelm him with temptation. Let him quarter for fifteen minutes, then walk him at heel until he calms down. After half an hour of heeling, give him another short run, but you must retain control. It's better that he works perfectly for quarter of an hour than if he runs amok for half a day.

When the urge to shoot becomes too great, put your dog up where he can see and hear nothing. Now it's your turn, so load up and shoot like a pro. You have nothing to do except concentrate on those birds, knowing your dog is resting up. If you have an older dog, you can work him (I always have Blue standing by) or just let your buddies' dogs do the business.

Chapter Ten: Your First Season

Do not give your dog any retrieves while the guns are blazing and other dogs are running around; it will be impossible to retain control in these circumstances. Send him when the guns have stopped and only for a simple retrieve where you know the exact location of the bird. Encouraging him to run or swim around free hunting is a sure way to undermine all his training.

Never send him for any bird falling into full view that you can easily pick yourself. Give him half a dozen such retrieves and he will break every time he sees a bird hit the ground.

Wait until you have a stone dead bird in light cover. This is just the kind of confidence-building work you both need. Remember, your aim is to develop teamwork so don't let him down. Make sure you have marked the fall

"I thought you had the gun."

Just another day at the office for this dog.

and know precisely where you are sending him. If you are not sure, send another dog. You don't want your dog thinking you're a jerk.

Build up the difficulty of his retrieves step by step, always working on his weaknesses. If he has a problem honoring, give him long periods of inactivity. If he lacks drive, build up his enthusiasm by sending him the moment a shot bird splashes down onto the water.

There is absolutely no point in giving your dog endless amounts of work he can do with his eyes closed. Coach him to do those things he finds difficult.

Currently I have three Labs in training waiting to go to new homes in America. Billy is a confident, boisterous

Chapter Ten: Your First Season

little chap who will run off into the distance to do his own thing given the slightest excuse. I make him walk to heel all the time he's out. He's not overly keen on swimming, so we work in the lake four times a week. He doesn't like water re-entries, so all his retrieves are on the far levee requiring him to do precisely that.

Harris is "Velcro Dog" and refuses to leave my side. I always save a few minutes of each training session and encourage him to run free. He loves to swim, so we only do water work once a week.

Sherry has the best nose of any female in the kennels and is mad to hunt. I train her as far away from game scent as possible. She hates to sit still, so I leave her on stay in the yard while I eat lunch.

With each of these dogs, I'm slowly strengthening their weaknesses — working on areas in which they already excel is a waste of time.

As the season progresses and your dog is less overwhelmed, you can increase his workload. Give him the odd cripple to track, but do it gradually and don't brag up the numbers.

You have no idea how disappointing it is to receive an e-mail from a client saying, "Beth is doing really well and has retrieved over seventy ducks in her first season."

I just know that next time we meet up, Beth will be completely self-employed and wild as a coyote.

I want owners to tell me, "Beth has had a careful introduction to her first season. She's only retrieved a handful of birds but is rock steady." That way, I'll know there is a very good chance Beth is on her way to being an excellent retriever and a joy have around. I can name hundreds of really smart, well-behaved twelve-month-old dogs, but only a handful smart, well-behaved of three-year-old dogs.

Make it your goal to have an obedient and competent adult dog rather than a flashy, hyped up-youngster. If you can resist the temptation to do too much too soon, you can do it.

Teamwork

I was at the checkout of my local supermarket last week. The spotty youth on the cash till inspected my charge card and without looking up asked, "You Vic Barlow then?" Rather pleased to be recognized I replied in the affirmative.

"You write for that magazine don't you?"

Bristling with pride I replied, "Yes, that's me."

"And all that radio stuff on Silk FM, you do that as well?"

"Yes I do."

"I thought I recognized your voice."

"Do you read my column?" I enquired, positively oozing celebrity status.

"No, but my dad does."

"I'm very pleased to hear it."

"You shouldn't be."

"Why not?"

"He thinks you're a jerk."

This was not what I wanted to hear but it was probably the truth.

Now your dog may not be as eloquent as Acne Boy but it doesn't mean he doesn't have opinions.

Chapter Ten: Your First Season

Once he genuinely knows what is expected of him his performance will be directly related to how much he wants to obey your instructions.

He may comply because he fears your response to a refusal and this works up to a point, but fear becomes less and less effective as the dog adjusts to your corrections.

As your dog matures and knows precisely what is expected of him, you must gain his respect. We have all heard owners complaining. "That dog is one headstrong son-of-a-gun."

Try and imagine what the dog's thinking: "He's waiving his arms up and down again. What the hell is that supposed to mean?"

Or worse still: "That's the third time today he's told me to look for a bird in the wrong place. It's better if I ignore him."

When your retriever doesn't respond correctly, most often it is because he doesn't understand what you want.

Don't think it doesn't happen. The more experienced the dog, the more he expects of you. You may like to believe that he worships the ground you walk on, but if you are a dimwit, he'll know it.

The thought pattern of a first-season dog is quite different to that of an old campaigner. If you screw up your early handling, a young dog can lose a lot of confidence. If you ask him to stop, cast right and hunt, and he finds nothing, he's likely to believe he's not doing it right. If he ignores you and moves in the opposite direction but still finds a bird, he will be convinced he doesn't need you.

Blue is my demonstration dog and I use him to illustrate to my Wednesday night class what we are striving to achieve.

Last week I left three bumpers in separate locations at the far side of the river in preparation for our lesson. Two hours later, I assembled the class on the levee and sent Blue to do his duty. He went off moodily in his usual "I'm only doing this until duck season" kind of way. When he reached the opposite bank, he stopped and asked me for directions. I raised my arm directly above my head and shouted "Get back." Blue knew I wanted the bumper directly behind him and off he went to retrieve it.

When I thought he'd gone far enough, I stopped him on the whistle. He looked back and I called "Hi-loss," his signal to get his nose down. He hunted for a while then turned his back on me and galloped off farther into the distance. I stopped him, blew the recall whistle, and insisted he hunt in the original location. He gave a cursory sniff then bolted away. I blew the whistle again and Blue spun around, giving me a look that suggested if I

Chapter Ten: Your First Season

were to stop him one more time he would come straight back and shove my stop whistle up my ass. Fortunately, Blue and I know each other inside out and if he's assessed the job and says I've made a mistake, I believe him.

I allowed him to hunt farther back and two minutes later, he swam back with the bumper and stuffed it unceremoniously in my hand. This was a case of pilot error; I'd forgotten the location of the dummy. Blue knew it and so did I. We are an experienced team; we've been around the block a few times and have learned to tolerate each other's mistakes, but you cannot do this with a young dog. If you are not certain where the bird is, don't send a first season dog — it's asking for trouble.

Here's a question to test your retriever training skills. If you send your dog for a bird and he refuses any

An older, experienced dog knows just about as much as you do about hunting.

attempt to handle him but still returns with the bird are you disappointed or ecstatic?

If you said "ecstatic," your dog is well on his way to running the show. At this stage of the game, obedience is more important than picking the bird. You should immediately re-run the retrieve and make him do what he's told. That way, you will both learn together.

As dogs mature, they learn your strengths and weaknesses as well as their own. If your dog is a really good marker, he will be easier to handle on a blind retrieve than on a mark where he thinks he knows best. If he doesn't have confidence in you, he probably won't handle on a mark at all.

Here are a few "secret" drills I've learned from some of Britain's best trainers. They are real team builders and work like magic on maturing dogs who think they know it all.

Pre-Season Tune Up
Regardless of the age and experience of your dog, you should always approach the new season as if he were a six-month-old puppy.
- Walk him on the leash at heel and blow the stop whistle, making him sit down immediately every single time.
- Set up simple left, right, and back drills in easy locations (not in cover), and make him execute them perfectly. Be picky and insist on total obedience.
- Leave him on stay, go indoors, and have a cup of coffee, but watch him through the window. Don't allow him to shuffle around.

CHAPTER TEN: YOUR FIRST SEASON

Review basic obedience drills as a pre-season tune up. Make your dog sit and be calm while you eat lunch, or sit still around other distractions.

- Fire shots and throw cold birds around him while he sits steady.

This should take about a couple of weeks for an older, experienced dog. Do not give him any difficult long retrieves while he is going through a pre-season tune up; simply treat him like a young dog just learning the ropes.

When you have him absolutely perfect, you can progress to the following.

The False Mark
Have a bird boy standing downwind throw a bumper and fire a shot. Your dog will believe that if he runs straight ahead, he will find a reward.

Send your dog, but stop him on the whistle half way. (If he keeps running, forget this drill and go back to teaching the stop whistle.)

Once he stops, count to ten, then cast him right where you will have already spread a line of birds he just can't fail to find. Not only will your dog have success, he will have exchanged the reward of a bumper for a plump juicy bird... excellent.

What do you suppose your dog will think now? He'll think you are a genius. Next time, take him to another spot, send and stop him, but this time cast him left. Lo and behold, he will find another bird. Now he's a believer. You are conjuring birds out of nowhere and in his eyes you are a saint.

You can't do this all the time or your dog will lose faith in himself, but for a headstrong dog, it's a great team-building drill.

Don't Fence Me In
Another effective routine you can use to win your dog's confidence involves an enclosed field. Before you bring your pupil out of the truck, go to the corner of the field where two fences meet, preferably one that is downwind, and throw several bumpers over the fence directly in front of you. (We will call that "Location 1.") Next, pitch several more bumpers over the barrier to your side (Location 2), then turn 180 degrees and walk fifty yards and drop several more in Location 3 (see Diagram 13).

Spread all the bumpers out at least five yards apart — we want to make it easy for your dog to walk right into one.

Collect your dog and walk him to the same corner and drop a bumper at his feet, then turn and walk him away. As you do so, have a buddy quietly pick up the bumper you just dropped.

Chapter Ten: Your First Season

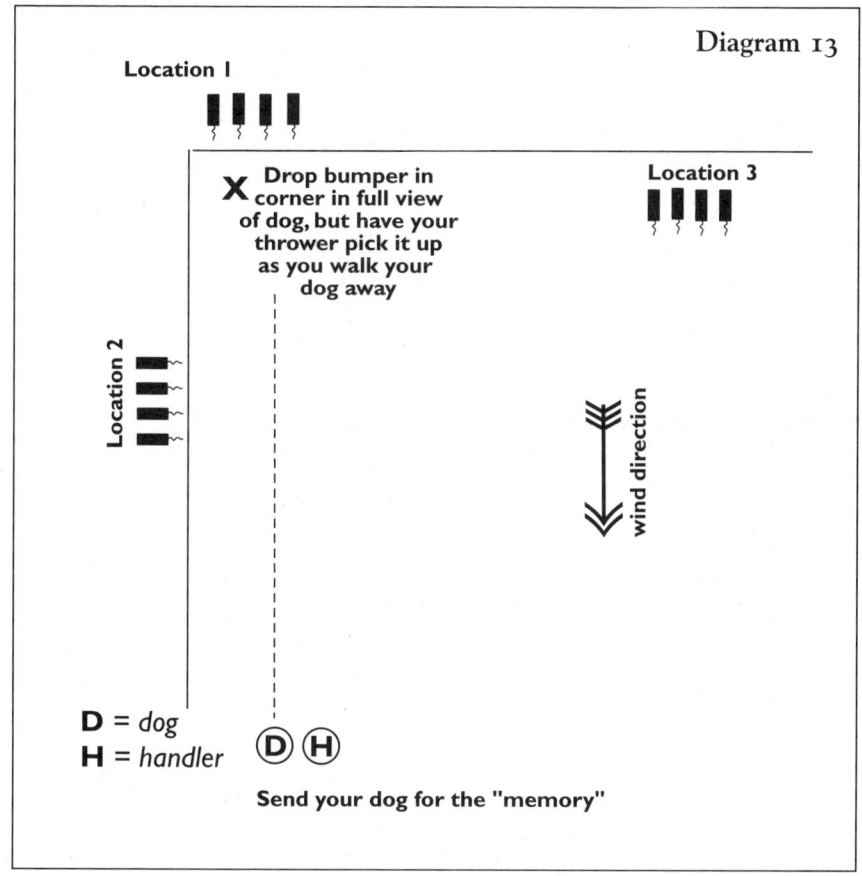

Set up your bumpers before taking your dog from the truck.

When you are 100 yards away (the distance is unimportant as long as you are confident your dog will respond to your commands), send your dog for the bumper he saw you drop in the corner. He thinks he knows exactly where to find it, but he will be wrong. When he has hunted the area for a minute, blow the stop whistle and order him to go back to Location 1. He will look at the fence and he won't believe you. He knows he saw you drop the bumper in front of the fence; nevertheless, insist that he goes back. Don't allow him to run around like a headless chicken. He knows what "Back" means and he must comply. Of course, when he leaps over the fence he will run straight into a bumper.

Now drop another bumper in the same corner. Have your buddy secretly pick it up again as you walk your dog away, then turn and send him back. When he realizes the bumper isn't there, he will want to go back to Location 1 as he did previously. Stop him and instead cast him to Location 2. Again he won't believe you, but don't allow him to run around. He has already been taught to cast and you must insist that he goes. The moment he complies, he will run into another bumper and will wonder just how the hell you do it.

On the final run, send him once more to the corner for the seen bumper (already picked up by your cooperative buddy), but this time stop him and cast him towards Location 3, where he has no barrier to cross. As long as he follows your directions, he will find another dummy.

His belief in you will have grown considerably during this exercise, but his self-confidence will need a boost, so drop a last bumper in the corner, walk him away, but *do not* pick it up. Turn your dog around and send him as before, but this time let him find the bumper exactly where he expects it to be.

Hunting Back

This drill works best along a straight path or track. Stand on the path with a bird boy standing upwind, directly fac-

Chapter Ten: Your First Season

ing you eighty yards away. Have him fire a shot and throw a bird.

Send your dog for the mark and as he reaches the half way stage, have a second bird boy drop another bird twenty yards behind him (see Diagram 14).

Before your dog reaches the first bird, stop him. Now blow your "Hunt back" whistle. He will not have seen the second bird down, nor will he be able to scent it and he won't believe you. He will naturally want to go for the first bird with the scent drifting towards him, but do not let him

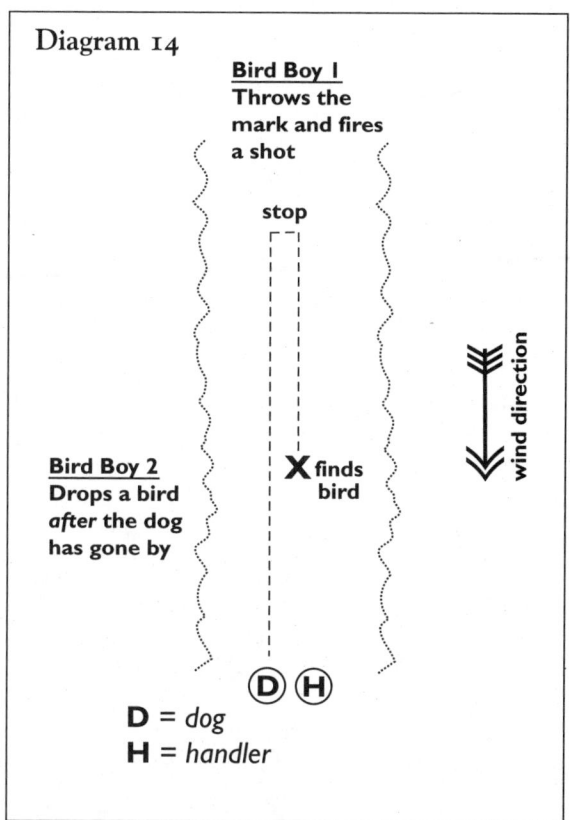

Teaching your dog to "Hunt back" on command.

have his way. Insist he obeys your "Hunt back" command and as he does so, he will walk right into the second bird.

The reason you are on a pathway is to encourage your dog to come back in a straight line and successfully find the second bird. This drill tends to fall apart in an open field as your dog can hunt back without finding the second bird.

Now change the location and run the same drill, but always end by giving him a straightforward mark.

With a little imagination you can run all these drills on water, but make sure your dog is already 100 percent on land before you try.

Think through the layout and the wind direction before your dog comes out of the truck. Most problems can be avoided with a little pre-planning.

Warning!

All the above drills are extremely effective techniques for developing your dog's confidence in you. They are intended for experienced dogs with lots of self-confidence, but are totally inappropriate for nervous young dogs lacking experience.

Even with older dogs, go back to basic drills, such as this typical walk-up line doing a marking drill.

CHAPTER TEN: YOUR FIRST SEASON

Blue always benefits from a team-building session at the start of the season, but he's a secure, experienced dog who knows his place in the world. Were I to run these with Harris, my "Velcro dog," they would destroy him. Harris is only eighteen months old, still learning his trade, and constantly looking for my approval. Running drills that prove him wrong would completely undermine his confidence.

These exercises are also totally inappropriate for teaching casting to a badly-schooled dog.

Use this information as your secret weapon to rebuild teamwork in your older, more experienced dogs who already understand all of the commands but are not eager to comply.

Working with an Experienced Dog
If there is one aspect of retriever training more rewarding than watching a pup develop, it's working with a well-trained, experienced dog.

I have learned more from older dogs than I ever have from books and videos. Many of the finished dogs I have acquired have been very good, some have turned out to be excellent, and the odd one or two simply gifted.

Of course I've had characters like young Grouse, the smartest son-of-a-gun I ever worked. He could master any new drill with few repetitions, and had he been equipped with a gun, would have dispensed with my services completely and ran the whole show himself. He challenged every decision I ever made.

We never really gelled as a team and when he was eventually sold to an Arkansas duck hunter, I waived him a fond farewell. An hour later, I spotted him and his new owner parked up by the roadside less than five miles from the kennels. (No doubt arguing about who should drive.)

Sweep, a handsome yellow Scottish Lab was a totally different personality. He'd already had three owners who had worked him hard with little or no appreciation and he had lost faith in people. He could tolerate other dogs, but people he could live without. Sue from San Diego fell in love with Sweep and took him home with her immediately. I wished her luck and hoped she received more attention from Sweep than I had.

Three months later they attended a workshop together where to my utter amazement, Sue and Sweep appeared joined at the hip like teenage lovebirds. Sweep had literally been swept off his paws.

When you take a good finished dog on a hunt, there are few surprises. He knows what's expected when those birds start falling. He's not going to lose his cool and run amok. He knows the rules and won't embarrass you.

He will, however, be watching you and measuring your expertise, and he won't be impressed if you miss mark or over handle him when he's taking care of business. If he's an ex-field trial dog (as most British imports are), he will undoubtedly test you to see if you intend to apply the exacting standards which he has been brought up to observe. He will undoubtedly adjust his behavior accordingly.

When you first acquire a finished dog, resist the temptation to rush out and work him. Spend a couple of weeks getting to know him. Walk him at heel and insist on dis-

CHAPTER TEN: YOUR FIRST SEASON

An experienced dog knows what's expected of him when the birds start falling.

cipline. Leave him on stay, and walk around him in circles. Go through all the basic training drills until you become acquainted with each other. This is where the mechanics of your relationship will be determined.

If you rush into the field before you have a rapport, you are inviting confusion and uncertainty. However you blow your whistle, it will be different to what he's used to. It's no good hollering "Dead bird" if he has no idea what it means. Maybe he responds to "Get out" rather than "Over." Spend some quality time developing your teamwork. He will respect you for it.

Some dogs will accept a change of ownership with little reaction but others can take a month to settle down.

Dogs can interpret your moods and read your body language better than any psychologist.

It's not wise to work a new dog in the field until he has learned to trust you. If he becomes fearful or confused, he may bolt and disappear over the horizon.

In my experience, age makes no difference to a dog's ability to form a bond. It's just as easy, sometimes easier, to build a good relationship with a five-year-old retriever as it is with a pup. Generally speaking, older dogs will settle with anyone who offers food and shelter, but will idolize an owner who provides leadership.

At the risk of repetition, you must be conscious of the ability of your dog to assess you. Placing all the responsibility on the dog for your relationship is a big mistake. If a hitherto well-behaved dog starts to misbehave, it's because he thinks you are weak.

Chapter Ten: Your First Season

Conversely, if you over discipline a sensitive dog, you may see his confidence collapse.

Take time to get to know each other and remember you can't fool him. He can interpret your moods and read your body language better than any psychologist. Be fair, firm, and strive to live up to his expectations. It will be worth the effort.

Chapter Eleven
General Health

An acquaintance recently left his two Labradors with me for a few weeks training. One dog, Bud, is already a Field Trial Winner and therefore of considerable value.

He's a big yellow handsome brute (the dog, not the acquaintance), and used to the best of everything. I was given specific dietary instructions, notes on how he should be kenneled, all his likes and dislikes, etc., etc. In fact, I was left more information for Bud than some parents leave for a baby.

His owner called every day to enquire about his welfare and discuss progress. Everything was going fine until the morning when Bud hobbled out of his kennel with a large lump on his hindquarters. It looked like someone had opened up his skin and inserted a golf ball. I was horrified.

While I was examining Bud, his litter brother, Chuck, trotted out of the kennel. I was totally preoccupied with Bud's mysterious lump and didn't notice Chuck steal my hand towel.

Bud's growth looked serious and I made a frantic phone call to my vet. The receptionist was very sympathetic and asked me to take the dog (and the lump) to the surgery for immediate examination. I was bundling Bud in the back of my truck when I suddenly spotted his kennel mate running around with the towel.

No matter how much I tried, Chuck absolutely refused to give it up, so I had a brilliant idea. If he wouldn't let me near him to retrieve my towel, maybe he would drop it and come running if I brought out a bitch.

I nipped back into the kennel and reappeared with Gabby, a beautiful young fox-red female, who immediately went straight over to him and rolled invitingly on to her back. I was totally unprepared for what happened next. Chuck took one look at her, stopped dead in his tracks, then swallowed the towel. Honest to God, no word of a lie, this stupid love-struck idiot gulped down an entire hand towel. I stood frozen to the spot in total disbelief.

As reality hit me, I began to wonder what the hell I was going to say to the owner?

"Yes, your dogs are fine, except for the one currently maimed by a large lump. . . And Chuck? Oh yes, his training is going really well. He's swallowing towels at the moment but don't worry, I should have him on swords by the end of next week."

Cold sweat was running down my neck when I arrived at the veterinary surgery.

"Is the vvvet in?" I stammered.

"Yes, it's the dog with the lump isn't it?"

"Err...Forget the lump."

"I don't think we should do that, it could be serious."

"I have an emergency."

"Yes, I know you told us on the phone. It's a lump like a golf ball."

CHAPTER ELEVEN: GENERAL HEALTH

"No, it's a towel."

"The lump's a towel?"

"No the lump's a golf ball. The other's a towel."

"The golf ball's a towel, the other's a what... I don't understand?"

"Look, it's simple. The big yellow one has the lump on the rump; the other, his brother, has a towel in the bowel."

"Mr Barlow, are you on some form of medication?"

Fortunately, at this point, my long-suffering vet appeared and saved me from men in white coats. With the calm authority born of experience, she listened to my incoherent ramblings and promptly stuck a few washing soda crystals down Chuck's throat and led him to the parking lot.

I cannot describe the relief I felt two minutes later when the towel reappeared, along with the entire contents of Chuck's stomach. I ran around cheer-

Beware of retrievers swallowing stuff.

ing and waiving a vomit covered hand towel in the air until I spotted a couple of worried veterinary nurses observing me from the surgery window. With the threat of psychiatric restraint still hanging over me, I calmed down and went back inside to discuss Bud's mysterious lump.

By now the veterinarian had determined the swelling to be no more than a large blood blister and was already tickling a tomcat, or whatever it is that vets do to male cats, when I took my leave.

I was totally drained and in a state of post-traumatic shock when the phone rang back at the kennels.

"How are my dogs?"

"Oh, err. . . fine. Yes, absolutely fine."

"They are not proving too much trouble I hope?"

"No. . . no trouble at all."

"Are you sure?"

"Yes I'm sure."

"Only I forgot to mention the big one, Bud, is prone to blood blisters."

"What?"

"And the other one, Chuck, tends to swallow stuff."

"Grrrrrrrrrrrrrrr!"

"Hello, Vic, are you still there? Vic, Vic what is it?"

"Aaaaaghhhhh!"

"Edith, Edith, call 911 on your cell phone. I think Mr Barlow's having some kind of a seizure"

Thankfully on that occasion there was no permanent damage, but retrievers do have a desire to work that overrides all their natural instincts. Many dogs are so focused that they will suffer terrible injuries and give no indication until the last bird has been picked.

CHAPTER ELEVEN: GENERAL HEALTH

Retrievers are foolishly impervious to exhaustion and will literally work until they drop. Do not wait for declining enthusiasm to tell you your dog is dehydrated or suffering from exposure.

Whilst I trust Blue's hunting skills implicitly in matters of his own welfare, his opinion isn't worth a damn. He would rather freeze to death than miss a duck. In this sphere of our partnership, I call all the shots. When I decide he's had enough, I call "Time Out." I don't solicit his opinion.

Retrievers are foolishly impervious to exposure and exhaustion and will literally work until they drop. No dog can be accustomed to the vast differences in temperature experienced across the North American continent and should be closely monitored for the effects caused by extreme conditions.

Do not wait for declining enthusiasm to tell you your dog is dehydrated or suffering from exposure. By this time, it may be too late to prevent long-term damage.

You are working as a team and your dog's welfare is entirely your responsibility. Your dog has the onerous task of repeatedly diving into freezing water or running down cripples in the heat of the day. He needs you to look out for him. Don't let him down.

Mutual Respect
If your dog was to steal the food from your mouth, snarl and show you his teeth or generally treat you as he would another dog, you would not be impressed, and neither will he if you treat him as a human being.

Attributing human characteristics to animals (anthropomorphism) is the preserve of Walt Disney. It's cute and funny, but totally inappropriate.

You may want to have a separate dog be the family pet.

CHAPTER ELEVEN: GENERAL HEALTH

Consider your retriever as a valued member of your family (pack) by all means, but also treat him as a dog. Failure to acknowledge this indisputable fact creates all kinds of problems for him and is a form of cruelty of its own.

Learn to read your dog. If he fails to respond to a command, try and determine if he is being obstinate or if he's simply confused, and tailor your reaction accordingly. He won't respect you for pussyfooting around after he's given you a stubborn refusal, and neither will he admire you for pressuring him to do something he doesn't understand. Losing your temper is such a bad idea that I won't bother reiterating the consequences.

Discipline yourself to be totally consistent at all times. Changing the rules depending on how you feel is a sure way to weaken your relationship.

If your family regularly takes your working dog to the park and fools around with him, don't expect him to be a top-flight gundog. He can't be expected to monkey around with other dogs, chase balls, entertain the kids, and still be a highly-disciplined retriever. If you want a "pet dog," adopt a mutt or at least make allowances in your dog's work ethic.

General Health Tips

Your dog's health is entirely your province and there is absolutely no excuse for leaving your dog outside without fresh water, shade, and shelter. Keep up with his shots and worm him regularly. Weigh him each month and set a maximum. Blue's working weight is sixty-five pounds; if he hits sixty, I increase his food; if he goes above seventy, I reduce it.

One of the best things you can do for your working retriever's hips and joints is to keep his weight down.

Make sure you have an emergency first aid kit in the truck. Also include some EMT gel in case of lacerations plus a clean towel.

Never ask your dog to work on a full stomach. Imagine his gut swinging and twisting beneath him as he runs and jumps. You can see how unwise that would be.

If you are consistent and create an environment where your dog can be totally confident of his role and status, you have the foundation for a great working relationship.

But to enjoy mutual respect you must *both* obey the rules. You are fifty percent of the partnership, that's the deal. Your dog can't do it all on his own. He needs you to pull your weight and you can be sure that he'll be watching.

Hips and Eyes

Retrievers are particularly prone to hip problems (dysplasia) and it is both irresponsible and immoral to breed from parents with poor hips.

When choosing a pup, you must ask to see the hip certification of both sire and dam. As dogs cannot be examined or certified until they are two years old, this is the only indication of your pup's future welfare.

There is no absolute guarantee that sound parents will produce litters totally free of hip dysplasia, but it is all you have to guide you.

As the dog matures, the effects of severe dysplasia can be clearly seen in his awkward gate as he tries to protect the weak joints. He will have difficulty negotiating stairs and although correct diet and exercise may give him a

Be careful with young pups' joints. Lift them down from the truck bed or other high places so they don't start their lives by stressing their hips.

long and happy life, he is not suitable for the high-energy activities of a gundog.

Not all hip problems are genetic. Many are the result of impact damage caused by too much early jumping. Take a look at the distance from your truck bed to the ground. It's a long drop for a young dog with soft bones. Given the amount of canine accessories available, I'm amazed no one offers a puppy ramp.

Of course, working retrievers have to learn to jump fences, gates, etc., but not continuously and certainly not before they are adults. If your dog is leaping out of your truck a couple of times a day onto a rock-hard surface, eventually his joints are going to suffer. Park on the grass and if you have a young or very old dog, put your arm underneath him and lower him down.

Above all, keep your dog lean and fit. Weigh him regularly and maintain his hunting weight. Don't allow his regime to become lax in the summer. It's not good to have his weight fluctuating wildly. It may work for Oprah, but not for a working retriever.

Cataracts

The most common eye problem is hereditary cataracts. All breeding stock should be eye tested and no one ought to consider buying a pup from parents who don't have current eye certification.

Severe forms of cataracts can require specialist surgery, which although normally quite successful can be very expensive.

Apart from hereditary genes, diabetes is also a known cause of cataracts, as is incorrect feeding in young pups,

CHAPTER ELEVEN: GENERAL HEALTH

It's impossible to tell if a pup will develop eye problems.

but with such excellent foods on the market, this should never occur.

Buying an Adult Dog

If you intend to purchase an older dog, your biggest difficulty will not be in finding one with good hips and eyes, but in simply locating the right dog for you. Well-trained, biddable, steady retrievers are a rare commodity requiring weeks of earnest searching (trust me, I know).

Unlike a pup, a serious hip problem in an adult dog will be obvious. He will be unable to perform the tasks expected of a hard-hunting retriever. If, as a result of extensive enquiries, you eventually find the right dog for you, spend some time working him. Watch him in action and have him jump a few fences and climb up and down a flight of steps. Handle him and put hand pressure on his joints. If he feels any pain, he'll soon let you know. Take a good look at his pedigree and check that his parents had good eyes and hips. If everything appears okay, take him home.

I have no idea what kind of hip joints Blue has. He is healthy, athletic, and never shows any discomfort. It's possible that his hip score may not be impressive, but as I don't intend to breed from him, it's irrelevant.

If working dogs are kept lean and fit, any minor shortcomings in their hip joints are soon balanced by their muscle tone. One of the biggest jumping Labs I ever saw had terrible hips, but she was kept fit and trim and never showed any discomfort at all, even when she was nine years old. Of course, she never had a litter of pups so her poor hips affected no one.

Eye problems can occur in any dog at any time. That's why eye certificates are only good for one year. So if your prospective dog appears to have clear eyes and jumps like a kangaroo, do the deal.

If, however, you intend to breed from your dog, then you must have good hips, current eye certification, and you will undoubtedly have to pay a premium price.

As a simple rule of thumb, if all you want is a good hunting dog, find a retriever that really impresses you and suits your needs. Give the dog a thorough work out, take him to the local vet for a medical if you wish, and if he looks and acts healthy, make him yours. All good kennels

Chapter Eleven: General Health

will give you a money-back guarantee that their dog has no known health problems.

If you aspire to be a breeder, finding a dog of your color, sex, and conformation with certified hips and eyes will be difficult enough. Don't turn down a dog just because it isn't a great performer or you may be waiting forever.

Top-flight working females with certified hips and eyes rarely change hands, and then only for exorbitant prices.

Chapter Twelve
Problem Solving

In 1974 I was an excited young man taking my very first walk on American soil, courtesy of Laker Airway's $99 New York Special. I had just checked in to a cheap and not very cheerful hotel in midtown Manhattan and decided to explore Eighth Avenue.

Garbage lined the sidewalk, producing the aroma of rotting fish, but here I was in the U.S.A. at last and nothing would prevent me from making the most of this God-given opportunity.

I nipped inside the doorway of a rundown store to shelter from the pouring rain and stepped on a bundle of humanity lying at my feet wrapped in several editions of The New York Times.

"Oh, I do apologize. I didn't see you there. Are you all right?" I asked in my very best British accent.

The Bundle sat up and rubbed a filthy mitten across bleary eyes.

"Can I get you anything?"

The Bundle just stared.

I bent down to his level to make myself understood "Are you unwell?" I asked in the manner one would address a young child.

Still no response.

He obviously didn't speak English so I switched to my best schoolboy French, the only other language I knew.

"Comment ca va? Etez vous malade ?" I enquired.

The Bundle gestured towards me. I leaned closer and he poked a stiff middle finger out from his grubby mitten.

"Yes, yes, what is it?" I put my ear close to his chapped lips, anxious to hear his words.

"Swivel," he hissed with liquor-laden breath.

"You're welcome," I replied, convinced it was some colloquial expression of gratitude.

The Bundle lay down and went back to sleep. I stuffed a couple of dollar bills into his coat pocket and continued my excellent adventure, deeply moved by the polite friendliness of New Yorkers.

It was years later when I found out that what I had taken to be a sign of appreciation had been nothing of the kind.

All retrievers, no matter how well trained, occasionally develop problems, which are almost always a result of poor communication. Let's make sure that you communicate better with your dog than I did with the tramp in New York.

Spinning or Popping

If your dog starts to spin or "pop" when you cast him, it is almost certainly due to lack of confidence. Many dogs that willingly blast off for a forty-yard memory pop when the distance is extended too far. If it is ignored in the hope that it will somehow rectify itself, popping becomes a habit, so don't allow it to develop. It doesn't look good and

Chapter Twelve: Problem Solving

A lack of confidence makes a dog stop in his tracks.

causes a break in your dog's concentration. No one wants to lose a bird while their dog is performing Swan Lake.

Shorten the distance until your dog regains his confidence and stops spinning, then build the degree of difficulty back up slowly. Rushing ahead too quickly is almost always the cause.

Occasionally, popping can come from over use of the stop whistle, causing the dog to slow down and turn around in anticipation of the command, but this looks quite different from the quick spin of the dog unsure of his task.

Make the drill you are working on easier and be patient. The aim is to build up your dog's confidence. When he knows precisely what he's doing he will not feel the need to pop.

Chasing

Chasing is a curse in any dog but in a working retriever, it spells disaster and can totally ruin a good day's hunting. The absolute best way to avoid this lies in your dog's early training regime. Do not let a young pup have free running in the mistaken belief that he needs to play. He can play just as well with you in the yard. In fact, he has a far better chance of developing a bond exercising with you than he does when left to rampage around on his own.

Once he learns the joys of chasing rabbits, squirrels, deer, etc., it becomes a really difficult problem to resolve. I've tried numerous ways of stopping dogs from chasing but I'd be lying if I didn't say that I've found intelligent use of the e-collar to be the most effective.

Max, my wife's golden, was crazy for rabbits. If he spotted one a mile away he was gone. He would run

Once a dog learns how fun it is to chase squirrels and other small animals, it becomes a really difficult problem to solve.

across roads, railway lines, anything to get to a rabbit. I tried bawling him out and shaking him after the event but to no avail. I even set him up and had my buddy release a rabbit in front of him and sacked him on his way out, but he just waited until the next time when I wasn't so prepared.

Once the chasing habit becomes established, only aversion therapy works and the timing has to be precise.

I could see that Max's rabbit obsession would eventually bring him to grief and I had to find a cure, which I did with the aid of an e-collar, zapping him the moment he gave notice to chase. Half a dozen tough sessions made him rethink his attitude to rabbits. Eventually, he began to give them a wide berth, but neither Max nor I enjoyed the experience.

If you want to avoid this unpleasant situation, never put your pup in a position where he is free to give chase. When he's steady, has learned to walk at heel and stop on the whistle, you will be able to manage his desire to chase with very little problem.

Obedience at a Distance

All retrievers learn that the farther you are away, the less likely you are to physically intervene should they disobey. Well-trained dogs that handle beautifully at fifty yards are quite capable of going deaf at 150. Progressing too quickly greatly contributes to this problem. You should stretch out the distance slowly while maintaining control.

Start each new season as though your dog is a six-month-old pup. Go right back to basics and don't accept anything less than perfection.

The farther away from you your dog is, the more likely he is to disobey.

Work through all your basic handling drills as though he is learning them for the first time, especially the stop whistle. Make him sit and stay while you go in the house for lunch and watch him through the window (be reasonable; don't leave him in direct sunlight or outside in a blizzard). If he moves, get out there and let him know it's not acceptable.

Drop a bumper in front of him as you walk him at heel and tell him to "Leave it." If you have a flushing dog, make him sit as you throw the dummy. Work your way through all his early training drills and extend the distance slowly. This way the necessity for you to go out 200 yards to correct him will be few and far between, but sometimes you just have to surprise him and do it.

CHAPTER TWELVE: PROBLEM SOLVING

Refusing Recall

Ignoring the recall whistle is more than just a refusal — it's an attitude problem. Your dog is telling you that he has little respect for your authority and is doing his own thing. This needs addressing immediately or his entire discipline will deteriorate.

Providing you are sure he can hear you (given the size of some American whistles, I can probably hear you), your dog *must* return. There are no acceptable excuses and he must be made aware of the price to be paid for disobeying. Whatever it takes, find him and drag him back towards you while blowing the recall whistle. Make sure you do it in such a way that he will not welcome a repeat performance.

Refusing the recall whistle is an attitude problem that cannot be tolerated under any circumstances.

Now deliberately send him to an area where there is plenty of scent to hunt, but no bird and recall him. If he stops hunting and comes back promptly, all well and good. But if he doesn't, repeat the previous correction, only this time with more vigor.

A word of warning: make absolutely sure that your dog fully understands the recall whistle and that his hearing is not impaired by running water, long grass, or unfavorable wind conditions. Disciplining him for something he doesn't fully understand can cause great confusion.

Handling in the Wind

Dogs do not like to run directly into the wind and will often refuse a cast they would otherwise take if it sends them head on into the wind.

My young dog, Daz, handles extremely well but will sometimes balk at being cast into the wind. Remember also that if your dog will run out one hundred yards for a blind downwind, he'll probably only go fifty yards in a headwind.

The only way to combat this is to train in windy conditions and make sure your dog always finds his bird when you cast him into the wind. You can do this by laying out half a dozen birds in advance so that when he does take the cast, he walks right into a bird. That way he will understand that battling the wind brings its own rewards.

Put Obedience First

Almost every amateur retriever trainer is bumper orientated and it's a fundamental mistake. You must train for *obedience* and if as a result, your dog comes back with a bumper, it should be viewed as a bonus. If your dog refuses your stop whistle but comes back with a dummy, it's a failure and should be treated as such. Your dog must be trained to take direction and work with you to achieve a goal. Success is seeing your dog respond correctly to direction. Don't be fooled into thinking the name of the game is finding a bumper. You can achieve that with an untrained dog. But you must play your part and be absolutely sure you know where the bird/bumper is to be found. You must prove to your dog that following your directions is worthwhile. Sometimes, it's wise to forgo the bumper and just make your dog do what he's told.

Y'all Come Back Now

Well, that's it folks. I'm just packing up all my gear, saying farewell to my good friends in Mississippi, and heading back to England. It's the end of another workshop.

Carol Gibson in Tupelo will welcome her deputy chief back home; Cathy Stewart at Wildrose Kennels can reclaim her guest room; and life all over the state returns to the weekday norm but not for me.

After months of burning the midnight oil I have finally reached the end of my first American book and I know it sounds weird, but I'm really going to miss you guys.

I've pictured working with you and your dogs every day since I began this project over a year ago, and now that it's time to wrap up, I'm reluctant to say goodbye.

In my mind's eye I can see Randy and Clint in Georgia working their Labs in the flooded timber, and Jimmy from the Delta trying to stop his mother petting on his dog.

I know there will be a "Chuck" somewhere in Tennessee saying "ain't nothin' gonna fix my dawg." And of course there's a "Larry" in New York longing to e-mail me as soon as my book hits the stores to tell me where I went wrong.

Sue in San Diego is probably married to Sweep by now, and the members of the Pin Oak Hunting Retriever Club will probably still be talking about the Arkansas tick that worked its way back to England in my butt.

I know Don and Stella in Illinois will be finding it

Email me and Blue, and tell us how you and your dog are doing!

impossible to stop treating their chocolate Lab as a substitute child, and I really don't want to spoil the illusion.

I never knew the name of the ginger-bearded giant who thought D.U. dog Drake was, "Just a little guy in a doggie costume," and I doubt he will ever read this book, but I still smile whenever I think of him.

I've had malts in Memphis, beer in Buffalo, Chardonnay in California, and whiskey in Tennessee so potent it would paralyse a grizzly. It's all been done in the name of retriever training. . . honest.

So now that it's time to leave, I just can't bring myself to go. How am I going to face the day without our regular training sessions? Who am I going to talk to when I hit the keyboard?

Usually the moment I enter my office in England, I'm in Maine, Texas, or Arkansas. I'm working with Frank and

Fred in the woods of Illinois or walking the beaches of Southern California showing Sue how to handle Sweep and I've loved every minute.

For the past year I've probably spent more time with you and your dogs than I have with anyone back home and now I just can't say "goodbye."

Look, I'll tell you what we'll do. E-mail me with a regular rundown on what you and your dog are doing. Tell me all your news, fill me in on the progress of your pup, and we can stay in touch.

If you want to attend a workshop or have me run one at your retriever club, just hit the keyboard.

You can reach me at vicb4sport@aol.com or fax me in England on: 44-1260-253502.

As my Southern friends always say, "Y'all come back now."

Ya'll Come Back Now

INDEX

AKC Field Trial 91, 93
aggression 39, 49
barking 39
birds, introducing 158, 159
birds, live 158
blind retrieves 148-154
boats 192, 193
breaking 155-156
breeders 23, 29
breeds 24-25
British Retriever Championship 16, 181
cataracts 236-237
chasing 49, 95, 101, 244-245
cheating 165
come command, see *recall command*
creeping (shuffling) forward 89-90, 103
cripples 158, 160, 162
decoys, introducing 186-187
delivery to hand 104-109
dense cover 177-178
destructive chewing 39
dead bird command 46-47, 82, 138-141
diet 36, 233-234
ditches 174-175
doubles 113
down command 87
duck blinds 192-193
electronic collars 69-73, 104, 165
equipment 68-69
false marks 215-216
finished dogs 23, 50-53
flushing 199-203
food in training 41, 45, 75
force fetch 104
Great Outdoor Festival 17, 31, 72
gullies 174-175
gun, introducing 46
handling 143-148, 185-186, 189
heel command 75, 76-81, 165-166

hip dysplasia 235-236, 238-239
hold command 104-109, 111, 158, 184
honoring 208
hunt back whistle 141-143, 218-220
hunt dead command 138
inclines 170-171
jumping 175
leadership 31-39
lining 165-170, 187-192, 202-203
marked retrieves 154-158
obstacle work 170-179
patience 102
pedigree 19, 23
place command 87-89
popping 242-243
praise 57-68, 75, 78
pressure 57-68, 75, 78
quartering 195-203
recall (come) command 43, 75-76, 82-84,
recall, refusing 126, 247-248
relieving on command 44, 53
returning 35
scent 173-174
shake command 126, 183-184
singles 111-113
sit command 75
spinning 242-243
started dogs 23, 50-53
stay command 75-76, 84-87
steadiness 94, 116-121
Stewart, Mike 47, 72, 167
stop whistle 129-134
swimming, learning to 121-127
switching 114-115, 186
upland hunting 198-199
walk-up 154-156, 158
water retrieves 115, 122, 125, 181-193
whining 90-93
Wildrose Kennels 47, 167
wind 171-172, 248